Feisty *Lydia*

MEMOIRS OF A
GERMAN WAR BRIDE

Edna Thayer

Enjoy!

Edna Thayer

Feisty Lydia

MEMOIRS OF A
GERMAN WAR BRIDE

Edna Thayer

Minnesota Heritage Publishing
2009

For more information, contact:
Minnesota Heritage Publishing
205 Ledlie Lane, Suite 125
Mankato, MN 56001
www.mnheritage.com

ISBN: 978-0-9794940-8-6

Library of Congress Control Number: 2009923537

Published by Minnesota Heritage Publishing

Printed in the United States of America
By Corporate Graphics, North Mankato, MN

First Printing

Edited by Dr. Kurt Burch and Betsy Sherman

Cover art by Kirk Ross, Lydia's grandson

Cover design by Lorie J. Giefer

To order books, or to schedule presentations or book signings,
visit: www.feistylydia.com
Or call 507-267-4588 or e-mail: info@feistylydia.com
Reseller discounts available.

Dedication

This book is lovingly dedicated to

Lydia Ross

And her family

Husband John

Son John Jr. and wife Diane Ross
Elysian, MN

Grandson Kirk and wife Lisa Ross
Great-grandchildren Karlie and Caleb Ross
Lakeville, MN

Granddaughter Christine and husband Stephen Paton
Great-grandchildren Ian, Evan, and Ayla Mae Paton
Woodbury, MN

Acknowledgments

Deepest gratitude goes to Lydia, her family, and friends for the delightful countless hours of interviews, without whose cooperation this book would not have become a reality.

Sincerest thanks go to Lydia's grandson, Kirk Ross, for his magnificent artistic talents in creating the sketch of his grandparents on the cover and for the illustration of the map of Germany.

Warmest appreciation goes to Ellen Bisping, and Lydia's granddaughter Christine Paton, who read the manuscript, gave glowing reviews and wrote endorsements.

The professionals in the publishing business are owed a round of applause for providing excellent coaching and support in this journey. The publisher, Julie Schrader from MN Heritage Publishing, provided exemplary assistance. Dr. Kurt Burch and Betsy Sherman were invaluable as they edited the manuscript. Thanks to Corporate Graphics for printing the book, and especially to Lorie Giefer who contributed her creative talents in designing the cover using Kirk's sketch and in the layout of the book, and to Barb Wandersee who provided excellent project oversight.

Heartfelt Kudos is given to my family. Daughters, Tamara Thayer and Brenda Eisenschenk, and granddaughter, Allison Cooney, reviewed and critiqued the manuscript. Husband, David, provided unending support and encouragement throughout this writing adventure.

Table of Contents

FUN MEMORIES FROM FRIENDS AND FAMILY

RETIREMENT YEARS

EPILOGUE

APPENDICES

Foreword

Memory is a child walking along a seashore.
You never can tell what small pebble it will pick up
and store away among its treasured things.

Pierce Harris

Living next door to Lydia and her husband, John, was always a delightful adventure. When my husband and I moved into our cabin on Lake Francis in the summer of 1976, John and Lydia Ross lived in the house to the east of us. With 15 feet separating our two houses, we were really close neighbors. Lydia was quick to extend her hospitality and frequently invited us into her home for coffee, goodies, and sociability. Whenever we needed to tell someone from Elysian where we lived, all we had to say was that we were in the house just west of Lydia. Everyone in this town of about 400 people knew Lydia, and they would smile. We remained neighbors for over 30 years.

Lydia regaled us often with the stories of her life in Germany and in America. Although her life included tragedy and death-defying situations, Lydia would tell the stories in an entertaining and positive manner. The story of her life begged to be written. This book contains 44 of the most memorable vignettes of Lydia's life. It is written with the hopes of capturing Lydia's feisty personality, her heart of gold, and her friendly nature. A little history is included to provide a glimpse of Germany at the time Lydia lived there.

This book is written in anticipation that you will enjoy reading the memoirs of Lydia as much as others have enjoyed hearing them.

Edna Thayer, Author

Prewar Years

in

Germany

Lydia, 13 months

CHAPTER 1

Born Feisty

*If Lidwina didn't have such a feisty spirit,
she never would have lived.*

Midwife in attendance at Lydia's birth

Lydia and her husband John enjoyed telling a story about her birth in a potato patch. Lydia would say:

I am my mother's first child. She was just seven months pregnant when she went to help pick up potatoes at the home of her dad's stepdad. When Ma jumped off the wagon, I decided I had been cooped up long enough and I decided to jump out, too. I was born right then and there.

John would add: "I think her ma picked up the wrong potato."

Actually, Lydia's mother did jump off the wagon and go into labor. She managed to walk home the couple of blocks from the potato patch to their house in Neuötting, Germany. The town is located about 60 miles east of Munich, near the Austrian border. Lydia was born with a midwife in attendance. Because Lydia was born two months early, she weighed only three pounds. The midwife told her mother that she better pray for Lydia to die, because she was so small and would have too many problems if she lived.

Lydia was born on July 10, 1925, to Alois and Emilie Weber. She was christened Lidwina Emilie Weber and was affectionately known by her friends as Lydia, or Liddy. Her father worked in an aluminum factory, and her mother worked in a laundry near their house.

Premature babies were cared for at home and not sent to a hospital at the time Lydia was born. Emilie took very good care of Lydia. She put her in a cotton-lined shoe box and placed her in the warmed oven of their wood-burning cookstove for an incubator. Lydia was placed toward the front of the warmed oven with the door open. Imagine how tricky it must have been to monitor the temperature of that oven so Lydia neither shivered nor baked!

Once, when Lydia was about three months old, Emilie placed her on a table to change her diaper. While Emilie was reaching for the diaper, always adventuresome Lidwina decided to explore her surroundings, and she rolled off the table. Lydia escaped the adventure unhurt. By then she was strong enough to survive. The midwife told Emilie that Lydia would never have lived if she were not so feisty. Lydia was full of energy and continued to be high-spirited throughout her life.

Alois and Emilie had six more children, each born about two years apart. They are Luise, Seigfried, Carl, Anna, Elfriede, and Adolf. Lydia is 12 years older than the youngest, Adolf.

GERMANY IN 1925

In 1925, the year Lydia was born, 75-year-old Paul von Hindenburg, became the first president of the German Republic to be elected by popular vote. Although Von Hindenburg was an excellent military leader -- he took command of all German forces in 1916 -- he was not as effective as a political leader and had trouble dealing with the profound economic and political difficulties that existed following the war. The country was bankrupt, and millions of people were out of work. By the time Lydia was born, Germany had begun to recover from World War I. Most Germans had food, homes, jobs, and hope for the future. However, the Great Depression hit Germany in 1930. Workers again faced unemployment and hunger, and poverty again became rampant. Germany also faced the economic burden of war repayments required by the Versailles Treaty, which ended World War I. In 1929 Germany agreed to the Young Plan, which scheduled the outstanding payments for war damages.

During the economic turmoil after World War I, Adolf Hitler became the leader of the Nazi party and organized an army of hoodlums known as the storm troopers. They fought communists and others who tried to break up Nazi rallies. In the Beer Hall Putsch in Munich, on November 23, 1923, Hitler led more than 2,000 storm troopers on a march against the government. The police opened fire and killed 16 Nazis. The plot failed, and Hitler was sentenced to prison for treason. At the time of Lydia's birth, Hitler had just been released. While in prison, he wrote Mein Kampf, which translates to "My War" in English. The book outlined his plan to conquer much of Europe. He blamed the Socialists, Communists, and Jews for Germany's problems. He espoused a dictatorship as the only way of saving his beloved country.

*Lydia at her confirmation around 1933
Pfarrkirche Catholic Church, Neuötting,
Germany where Lydia was baptized, had First
Communion, was confirmed, and married*

CHAPTER 2

Attending School in Germany

School days, school days
Dear old golden rule days.
Readin' and 'ritin' and 'rithmetic
Taught to the tune of the hickory stick.

Will D. Cobb, 1907

During the time that Lydia attended grade school, it was not uncommon for teachers to "enhance" learning with the use of a stick. Although the above lyrics were written in America, the custom also prevailed in Germany.

Lydia was a petite, happy-go-lucky, spirited child. When she was two years old, she started kindergarten, which she attended until she was six. Her father would put Lydia inside his backpack and pedal her to kindergarten on his bicycle.

At age six, Lydia started first grade. She completed eight grades of school. In those days, an eighth-grade education was the norm for both boys and girls. Lydia enjoyed school, and her high spirits were always on display. She remembered marching outside with her class one day, with the nun who led the group at the front. Tiny Lydia was marching in the last row, happily singing a little tune as children will do. She thought the nun was too far away to hear her. The words rhymed in German. Translated, they were:

Left, right, left, right
Behind the teacher who stinks.

The nun heard Lydia and asked her to come to the office. She did not hit Lydia with a stick, but she punished her by requiring her to kneel on a piece of wood for an hour. When Lydia returned home that day, she had such deep grooves in her knees that her mother went to speak with the nun. Lydia said her parents always supported the teachers, but that time was an exception.

Another vivid memory from Lydia's schooldays was of standing in the woods when a Hindenburg Zeppelin flew overhead. Lydia said it flew so low the schoolchildren were afraid it would hit the church steeple and explode. Luckily, it missed.

GERMANY FROM LYDIA'S BIRTH TO WORLD WAR II

Paul von Hindenburg appointed Hitler as Chancellor of the government in 1932. When Hindenburg died in August 1934, Hitler was already ruling the country. Hitler gave himself the title Fuehrer, or leader. By July 1933, the Third Reich had outlawed all freedom of the press, all labor unions, and all political parties except for the Nazis. Propaganda filled the nation. After 1938 Hitler decided where people could work and what they could earn. Anyone who opposed him could be executed. Hitler was determined to avenge Germany's defeat in World War I, and in open violation of the Versailles Treaty, he prepared the country for war. Fearing another world war, no other nation stopped him or tried to oppose him. Hitler absorbed the Rhineland, Austria, and Czechoslovakia. When German tanks rolled into Poland on September 1, 1939, Britain and France declared war on Germany. World War II had begun.

CHAPTER 3

A Year in Munich

We do not remember days; we remember moments.

Cesare Pavese

Lydia was 14 when she completed eighth grade. The German government required all 14-year-old girls to live with a family selected by the government, to learn how to cook, clean, and keep house. The boys were required to spend one year on a farm. Lydia lived with a family in Munich for a year from 1939 to 1940.

Hitler visited Munich in the summer of 1939. The town was full of excitement. The family with whom Lydia lived took her to the big building with arches where Hitler spoke. Afterward, Hitler came into the crowd and shook Lydia's hand. It was the thrill of a lifetime! Hitler kissed the hand of her friend, and she did not wash her hand for several days. Hitler was popular at this time. One of the things that Lydia's family liked about the government was that it gave families a certain amount of money for each child that they had. With their seven children, the money helped Lydia's family survive the years of poverty.

In Munich, Lydia earned five German marks a month. The deutsche mark, or German mark, was the equivalent of slightly more than a dollar in American money. The family provided her food and housing so she was satisfied with her salary. Although the family wanted her to stay longer, Lydia missed her own family and decided to go home. She attended beauty school for a year in Altötting, about three miles from Neuötting.

*Lydia's parents with three of her brothers and
two sisters at their home in Neuötting*

GERMANY

AT

WAR

CHAPTER 4

Boosting the Soldiers' Morale

What a wonderful thing is the mail, capable of
conveying across the country a warm human handclasp

Rajan Bakshi

Among Lydia's memoirs is a photo album containing pictures of many of the soldiers to whom Lydia wrote during the war. Lydia met many soldiers while in beauty school, when she had time off from the munitions plant, and later through her work with the medic unit and at The Club, a German guesthouse in Neuötting. Her husband, John, says with a twinkle in his eye, "Lydia was a real flirt." She was cute and petite with a perky personality. Lydia always said she was just trying to boost the soldiers' spirits by flirting, but she would not let them get fresh with her. One night when a soldier made unwanted advances, Lydia stopped him and said, "Why would you do that?" He said the guy Lydia was with the night before had said she was really "great." Feisty Lydia demanded that the soldier take her to the man, who happened to be his commanding officer. Lydia marched up to the officer and asked, "Did anything happen between us last night?" The officer, red-faced, admitted that nothing did. "Then why did you say it did?" Lydia assertively demanded. The officer tried to explain: "Guys like to brag about things, whether or not they are true." Lydia told him emphatically, "Don't you ever lie about me again!"

Lydia wrote letters by the hundreds. The postage on letters to soldiers was free. Lydia believed that receiving letters would boost the morale of the young men. She told them she would be waiting for them when they returned. She often repeated the same words to several recipients. It was easier than trying to think of something new to say.

Once, Lydia wrote the same words in separate letters to two soldiers who happened to be in the same unit. They were next to each other as they were reading the letters. They began to compare and realized what had happened. Whoops!

CHAPTER 5

Riding a Tank to Italy

It's no use to cry and complain,
It's just as cheap and easy to rejoice.
When God sorts out the weather and sends rain,
Why, rain's my choice.

James Whitcomb Riley

Keep your fears to yourself, but share your courage.

Robert Louis Stevenson

When Lydia was 16, the German government began requiring each business establishment to send an employee to work in a munitions plant or join the army. Lydia, as the beauty school's newest employee, was selected to fulfill the requirement. Lydia did not want to join the army, so she chose working at the plant. It was outside the town of Kreiberg, about 60 miles west of Neuötting.

In 1942, while working at the plant, Lydia had earned some vacation time, so she and her friend Erna, whom she had met in Kreiberg, decided to take the train home to Neuötting. On their way back to work, they had to transfer trains in Mühldorf. There were some shiny new German tanks on a train on another track. When they went down to the tracks to look at them, a soldier inside one of the tanks invited them to climb inside and look around. Being adventuresome, they agreed. Just after they got inside the tank, the train started to move. They were scared to death. They had no money or belongings with them, although they did have their German ID cards, which they always carried. Erna bawled all the way, and Lydia told her to quit crying because it would do no good.

The train rumbled on and on. After what seemed like an eternity, it stopped. They had crossed Austria to the south and were at the Italian border. Erna and Lydia started to climb out of the tank, only to be met by the police. They were arrested and taken to a jail. Understandably scared, they wondered what would happen to them. That night Erna kept crying while Lydia tried to get some sleep.

The police must have believed their unusual story because in the morning they permitted the girls to take the train to Kreiberg. They had some money to pay for the train, because the soldier who had invited them to climb into the tank gave them some bills when they left and said, "Here, take this, you might need it." And indeed they had.

CHAPTER 6

Escaping Death

Although the world is full of suffering,
it is also full of the overcoming of it.

Helen Keller

The new, state-of-the-art munitions plant near Kreiberg was built entirely beneath a forest to hide the work area. The employees lived underground, too. Lydia had a bicycle and was permitted to leave the plant when she was not working.

Lydia had been working at the plant about two years when she met a German soldier on one of her rides into town. He was stationed on a submarine out of Bremerhaven and was home on furlough. They met each other several times. Before returning to his ship, the soldier convinced Lydia to take a day off work and join him on a picnic. Lydia, always a conscientious worker, worried about missing work, but something compelled her to join the soldier.

At noon on a bright sunny day, while Lydia and her friend were enjoying a picnic on the hillside overlooking the forest of trees covering the munitions plant, the sky suddenly seemed to darken with a group of planes flying low over the area. She said to her friend, "Oh, look, the Germans have some nice shiny new planes." The planes were flying so low, that Lydia could almost see the faces of the pilots in their cockpits. The soldier said, "Those aren't German planes; those are American planes." Just then the bottom seemed to drop out of the planes, and bombs began to fall on the forest above the munitions plant. The sky filled with clouds of smoke and fire from the explosions. Every person inside the plant was killed! No one came out alive. Lydia's observation: "Don't tell me it doesn't pay to play hooky!"

All Lydia had left were the clothes on her back and her bicycle. The rest had been destroyed. Lydia and her friend went to his mother's home in Kreiberg. Lydia's friend wanted her to stay, but Lydia decided to return to her own home, so she left the next day. She pedaled her bicycle the 60 miles back home. As she rode, she passed by the "camp" outside the city of Dachau. She wondered what type of prison was behind those walls.

Lydia pedaled as fast as she could. Sometimes she tired and walked beside her bicycle. She had no access to a telephone to call home nor any money or food. Lydia did not stop to eat and did not remember stopping to rest. If she did rest, it would have been only a catnap in the ditches alongside the road. Bicycles were much slower then, and it took her two and a half days to travel the 60 miles to reach home.

Meanwhile, news of the bombing had spread rapidly across the countryside. Lydia believed her family may even have heard the explosions or seen the smoke in the sky. The word that spread like wildfire was that no one had lived. Lydia's family expected the worst.

Imagine what must have gone through Emilie's mind when she saw her daughter coming through the door. Was it a ghost? Was it a mirage? Was it Lydia's spirit? She was thrilled when she realized it was really Lydia, tired and hungry, but very much alive!

When Lydia walked into the house, a German officer was sitting at the table. Lydia pointed to the door and told him emphatically to get out. The officer said he could have her and her family shot for telling him to leave. Lydia replied that the Americans would shoot them if they discovered him in the house. Because she was so insistent, he left. Lydia told her mother never to harbor a German soldier again or they could get in trouble from the Americans who were occupying the area.

Munich was also heavily bombed. Because of the bombing at the plant and in Munich, Lydia never knew how her soldier friend made it back to his submarine at Bremerhaven. But he did return to his ship. because she received letters from him later.

KREIBERG AND DACHAU

The United States entered the war in December, 1941. This bombing of the munitions plant occurred in early May of 1943, when Lydia was 17.

Kreiberg apparently no longer exists. It cannot be found on any current maps of Germany and is not included in an extensive listing of 2,075 cities in Germany. Both John and Lydia were certain of the name, spelling, and location of the town. Although the munitions plant was outside the city, perhaps the bombing exacted too great a toll on the city for it to survive.

The camp at Dachau that Lydia passed on her way home had opened on March 22, 1933, about two months after Hitler was sworn in as Chancellor of Germany. It had been in existence for 12 years when the U.S. Seventh Army liberated it on April 29, 1945. After Hitler came into power, the "enemies of the state" were arrested and quickly filled the existing prisons to overflowing. Additional "camps" were rapidly constructed to house them. Dachau was the first concentration camp built. Its first prisoners included Communists, Social Democrats, trade union leaders, spies, resistance fighters, religious dissidents, common criminals, Gypsy men, "asocial" people, and homosexuals. Others deemed undesirable, such as the elderly and disabled, who were thought to weaken Germany, were later added.

Although Jews were sent from the beginning, it was not because they were Jews, but because they were in one of the other categories. The Jews declared a holy war against the Nazis in 1938, and the first Jewish people taken into "protective custody" at Dachau because they were Jewish were arrested in November

1938. Catholic priests and Protestant clergymen who opposed the Nazi regime were added to the list of inmates in 1939.

Germany invaded Russia in 1941, and many Russian prisoners of war were sent to Dachau. The Russians were at a disadvantage at first because they were short on rifles. The rifles went to those at the front of the line, on the theory that the soldiers who followed could take them from the dead or wounded. As a result, many Russian soldiers were captured.

Several types of medical experiments were conducted on the concentration camp inmates, causing many deaths. Starting in February 1942, most of the Jewish prisoners in Germany were transported to the gas chambers at the concentration camps in Majdanek and Auschwitz, in Poland. In April 1942 a brick building was constructed in the woods next to Dachau. It held the gas chamber shower, a gas disinfection area, and four cremation ovens.

Despite its atrocities, Dachau was classified as one of the better camps in terms of its treatment of prisoners. It was never intended to be a camp for Jews. The reason there were so many Jews at the camp when it was liberated was that the Jewish camps to the east in Poland and Germany were liberated first, and those Jews were transported to camps further west. Many went to Dachau.

CHAPTER 7

Hometown at War

It isn't about waiting for the storm to pass,
It's about learning to dance in the rain.

Anonymous

When Lydia returned home after the explosion at the munitions plant, she found Neuötting invaded, with evidence of war all around. One group of Americans was stationed across the Inn River from her house. There had been a beautiful bridge across the river connecting Austria to Germany. The Germans blew up the bridge to prevent the Americans from crossing the river, but they came anyway in boats. The Americans arrived in Neuötting in May 1943. Lydia said she would never forget it because, unusually for southern Germany at that time of year, it snowed. Years later, after she moved to Minnesota, she wondered if the Americans had brought the snow with them to Germany.

The Americans walked each street and searched all the houses. Lydia and a group of her friends saw one American kick a man who looked like a German civilian. The man kicked the American back, and the American shot him. When he rolled the dead man over, she saw that he was a high ranking Hungarian with the SS army. He had his uniform on underneath the civilian clothes. The American may have caught a glimpse of the uniform before he shot the man. Lydia does not like to recall this event. She said it was what happens during war.

Food was in short supply, and the government rationed much of it. Fortunately, Lydia's family had a garden. Vegetable sandwiches were among the many things they learned to eat from items grown in the garden.

Strict curfews were set for 7 p.m. Military police patrolled the area and could arrest anyone found outside after curfew. Planes flew overhead searching for bombing targets. Munich was frequently hit. When the air raid sirens blared, families went outside to sleep the rest of the night in bunkers.

A German air force lieutenant dress uniform hung in Lydia's closet. It had been given to her by Otto, a soldier she had met when she was 15 and attending beauty school. He waved to her from a hospital that she passed by every day. She finally went inside to meet him. He left the uniform with Lydia when he departed with his unit to Italy and could not take it with him. When the American soldiers inspected her house, they opened the closet, saw the uniform, threw it on the floor, and stepped on it. Feisty Lydia picked it up and hung it back in the closet. The Americans took it out again and stomped harder on it. Even though the Americans spoke only English and Lydia spoke only German, she got the message. She waited until the soldiers left the house to brush off the uniform and put it back in the closet.

Many troops passed Lydia's house. The main road into the town had arches on both sides, making it too narrow for tanks and equipment to pass through. The alternate route passed Lydia's house. Lydia, afraid the troops would search their house again, decided to get rid of the uniform. Since postage was free on items shipped to military personnel, she later mailed the uniform back to Otto, who had been transferred from Italy to Berlin.

CHAPTER 8

Hungry Adolf

One of the oldest human needs is having someone to wonder where you are when you don't come home at night.

Margaret Mead

This story happened when Lydia's brother Adolf, nicknamed Adi, was six years old. He was 12 years younger than Lydia and he was always hungry.

One day, as American tanks rode past Lydia's home, a black man called out to Lydia flirtatiously, "Hello, baby." Lydia had never seen a black man before and did not really know what to think. The tanks rolled on into the nearby woods, where the soldiers camped for the night.

Adolf had not come home by 7 p.m. Emilie asked Lydia to find Adolf. Lydia was apprehensive, but she took her bicycle and left. As she pedaled past the woods, Lydia called for Adolf. He answered, saying he was with the American troops. Lydia told him to leave right away and come home. Adolf refused saying, "They're feeding me, and I'm not leaving until I eat." They offered a plate to Lydia, but she would not take any food. Lydia said one of the soldiers had a cross on his hat, and she thought he might be a member of the clergy. She felt a little better after seeing that. Lydia waited outside the camp for Adolf to come to her.

When Adolf finished eating and left the camp, Lydia gave him a ride. She told him, "Ma's going to give you a good licking when you get home." Adolf did get a hard spanking when he reached home, but he was content because he went to bed with a full stomach. Luckily the Americans moved on the next day, or hungry Adolf might have gone back to them again.

Brother Adolf, 12 years younger than Lydia

CHAPTER 9

Finding Work

When you get to the end of your rope,
tie a knot and hang on…and swing!

Leo Buscaglia

After the munitions plant was bombed, Lydia desperately needed a job. In 1944 she went to the mayor of Neuötting to inquire about work. The mayor had just received a request for help from an American medic group stationed in the schoolhouse where Lydia had attended school. The medics wanted two German girls to work in their kitchen, which was within walking distance from Lydia's home. After discussing it with her mother, Lydia decided to apply. Lydia and her friend Aemme were both hired.

Lydia and Aemme were treated well by the medic troops. They allowed the girls to take leftover food home to their families. Adolf, came by every day to see what might be left over. One day the German girls made a large batch of goulash, which the Americans did not like. Lydia asked if she could have the leftovers. When Adi came by as usual, Lydia sent him back home to get a huge container and his wagon. Lydia's family took what they wanted and had enough left to share with many of the neighbors. Lydia said she could still smell the simmering goulash as she walked through the streets the next morning.

Lydia met a kind American soldier from the medic troops and went out with him until the troops moved to another location. Lydia began to learn to speak some English, although she could understand more than she could speak. Lydia was amused by how much the Americans smacked their gum. She had never seen chewing gum before.

Lydia and Aemme worked in the kitchen until the troops moved on to a different location. The officer wrote a letter of recommendation for the girls to give to the new mess sergeant when the next group arrived to occupy the schoolhouse.

CHAPTER 10

Extra Mouths to Feed

With them I gladly shared my all and learned the great truth that when God guides, He provides.

Frank N. D. Buchman

Cologne, a large city several hours northwest of Neuötting, was heavily bombed during the war. In 1944, a busload full of children was brought to Neuötting to see if the residents would take them into their homes to escape the bombing. The kids were not orphans, but it was not safe to live in Cologne. The plan was to re-unite the children with their families after the war.

Lydia's family hardly had enough food for themselves, but Emilie went to see the kids. She wanted to help, even though she knew it would be difficult.

The last child standing by the bus was a young boy with blue eyes and blond hair. Emilie could not resist him, and brought him home. He stayed about a year with Lydia's family until the war ended, and it was safe to return to Cologne.

In April 1945, some German guards from one of the concentration camps walked a group of Jews through Neuötting on the way to Dachau. The war was almost over, and Lydia believed the guards may have been trying to hide the Jews. They went to the woods to camp.

When the group left camp the next morning, one of the boys was so weak that he fell down. The group went on without him. Lydia's mother found him and took him into their home, despite

Lydia's protests. When he came to the house, he was 18, but he was so thin they thought he was about 14.

He stayed about a month. During that time, the war ended. He went on to the city of Altötting where many Jews settled. He opened a barbershop in the same building where Lydia had attended beauty school.

DEATH MARCHES

The Jewish boy rescued by Lydia's mother was on a death march to Dachau. Lydia never learned which camp he left. As the Soviets rapidly advanced westward, the German army and SS units abandoned the death camps in Poland.

German police chief, Heinrich Himmler, ordered the evacuation of all prisoners toward the interior of the Reich. Jewish survivors were brought back to Germany to be crowded into the concentration camps at Bergen-Belsen and Dachau.

Historians believe Himmler issued the order because he did not want the prisoners telling their stories to the enemy and because the German army needed the prisoners' labor to maintain the production of armaments. Also, some officials believed they could use the prisoners as hostages to bargain for a separate peace to guarantee the survival of the Nazi regime.

The term "death march" was probably coined by the prisoners themselves because of the many who died along the way. The SS guards had strict orders to kill prisoners who could no longer walk or travel. Many died of exposure, starvation, or exhaustion.

Typhus, which had become an epidemic in the concentration camps, also caused many deaths. Typhus is caused by the rickettsia parasite and is spread mainly through body lice, and also through fleas, mites, and ticks. American soldiers were vaccinated for typhus, but the Germans had been unsuccessful in developing a vaccine. The only way they knew to kill the bug was to use the disinfection gas chambers.

The Jewish boy who dropped in the woods may have been presumed dead. He may have faked death. Or perhaps the guards thought he would soon die and just left him behind. He was fortunate that he was not shot.

Lydia in Germany about the time she met John

POSTWAR YEARS

IN

GERMANY

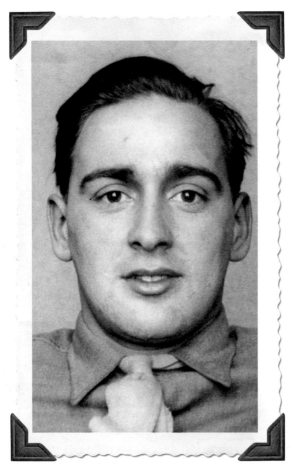

John Ross when he landed at
Pfaffenhofen, Germany, in 1944

CHAPTER 11

Meeting John

I'm going to get that man.

Lydia Weber

I'm going to marry that woman.

John Ross

Sergeant John Ross, who lived on a farm near the small town of Elysian, Minnesota, arrived in Pfaffenhofen, Germany, in 1944. The town is located about 66 miles northwest of Munich. John was assigned as the chief mess sergeant for an artillery unit that supplied food and ammunitions to other units. In 1945, after the war had ended, his unit was sent to occupy the schoolhouse recently vacated by the medics in Neuötting. Lydia and Aemme took their reference letter and went to see if they could find a job with the new unit. Lydia gave the letter to one soldier who gave it to John. He met the girls and said, "Sorry, no women in my kitchen." He had already requested and received seven German prisoners of war to be assigned to his kitchen, and he did not need any more help.

Rejected and disappointed, Lydia and Aemme left. Lydia said, "I'm going to get that man!" She meant she would get even with him.

Lydia must have displayed her feisty, high-spirited personality. As she left, John turned to his friend and said, "I'm going to marry that woman."

Hitler committed suicide on April 30, 1945. The war in Europe ended on May 2, 1945. John remained in Germany until the spring of 1948.

ELYSIAN

John's home town of Elysian is in south-central Minnesota, about 70 miles southwest of Minneapolis. The town was named in 1884 for the Elysian Fields, which in Greek mythology means Islands of the Blessed. Good souls were sent there after death if they had led pure lives. The Elysian Fields were a land of song and sunlight, where the air was sweet and cool. The good souls lived there in simple joy among the flowers and meadows. The town was named in honor of loved ones who had been killed in the Civil War.

The population of Elysian in the late 1940s was around 400. It later dropped to about 300, but is now around 550 because the city annexed a geographical area larger than the original area of the city of Elysian. The annexed area contains homes and people on the north side of town, around lakes and in housing developments, and included the lake home of John and Lydia Ross.

CHAPTER 12

Working at The Club

*Whenever we look upon this earth,
the opportunities take shape within the problems.*

Nelson A. Rockefeller

The Club was a German guesthouse across the street from the schoolhouse where John was stationed. The Club had been taken over by the Americans, but was still run by a German manager.

As Lydia and Aemme walked dejectedly from John's kitchen after being turned down for a job, they were met by two American soldiers, who asked if they were looking for work. When they replied that they were, one soldier said he wanted a girl to work at The Club, and he pointed to Lydia and said he wanted her. Lydia said she would have to ask her mother for permission.

Desperate for income, Emilie said Lydia could try working at The Club. The place had a reputation for rowdiness, and Emilie said that if it got too rough, Lydia could always quit.

Lydia had begun working at The Club when the manager approached her to ask if she were married. She told him no, and he said she could not work there because he hired only married women. As Lydia was removing her apron, the American soldier who had asked her to work there entered and asked why she was leaving. When Lydia told him, he grabbed the German manager by the neck and told him that Lydia was to be allowed to work. Lydia does not know why the American was so insistent. Perhaps he thought her feistiness would be an asset to The Club.

Lydia liked her work. She served beer. She heard that John often brought leftover food to The Club to be served there instead of throwing it away. Once John ground together Spam, cheese, and pickles and made sandwiches. The American soldiers ate very little at the mess hall, so he brought them to The Club, where the same soldiers enjoyed them. It must have been the different atmosphere. Perhaps they tasted better with beer. Lydia hoped to see John again, but she seemed to keep missing him when he came.

CHAPTER 13

Meeting John Again at The Club

Sweetest music to a woman's ear is that made by another woman playing second fiddle.

Dian Ritter

John was a good-looking soldier. Lydia always wondered if she would see him again after he turned her down for a job in his kitchen. Every day at work she searched the crowd of American soldiers to see if she could see John's eyes.

When John finally did return to The Club while Lydia was working, he was accompanied by another German girl. Lydia was happy to see John but was disappointed to see him with someone else. John was surprised and happy to see Lydia. He kept coming back to The Club alone, and he wanted to go out with Lydia, but she was wary about going out with him. The German girl was so jealous and angry that John was coming to The Club to see Lydia that she hit her in the face. This was all Lydia needed to make her realize that if John was worth fighting over, he was worth dating. They found that they enjoyed each other's company.

John was stationed at the schoolhouse for about six months before being sent to Munich. Not wanting to leave Lydia, he found a job for her at a club in Munich, as well as a nice room in a private home where she could stay.

John traveled often. His unit was responsible for providing supplies to other units, and because he spoke some German, he was often required to accompany people to other countries. John had learned German from the prisoners who had worked in his kitchen, and he continued to learn German from Lydia.

CHAPTER 14

Remembering

Don't brood on what's past,
but never forget it either.

Thomas H. Raddall

It was an unusually warm and humid summer day in 1945. The war in Europe had just ended. Lydia remembers it well.

General Dwight D. Eisenhower was the Supreme Commander of the Allied Forces. When he discovered the atrocities of the Holocaust he ordered a plan of action so that people would always remember. All possible photographs were to be taken and preserved. Residents of surrounding villages were ushered past some of the dead and told to bury them.

Holocaust is a Greek word which means, sacrifice by fire. Hitler believed the German people were a superior race, and he wanted to destroy people who he believed were inferior. He killed around six million Jews, approximately two-thirds of the Jewish population in Germany at the time. He also targeted other groups killing millions of disabled, homosexuals, Russians, clergy, and others. Although Holocaust means sacrifice by fire, he used gas, torture, and starvation in his death camps. Many died of disease. The dead were usually burned in a massive crematorium.

Lydia recalled American soldiers and German Jews coming to Neuötting and ordering the villagers to go to the town cemetery, which was about one mile outside of town. She could never have been prepared for what she was about to encounter. There were six victims from nearby Dachau laid out on the ground. The villagers, including Lydia and her family, were forced to walk past the badly decomposed bodies. Flies swarmed and the stench was overwhelming. Lydia attempted to cover her nose and face with a handkerchief, but the odors seeped through. One of the Jewish men removed the handkerchief from Lydia's face so she would get the full effect. The fumes burned her eyes.

When the same Jewish man who removed Lydia's handkerchief saw Emilie, he told her she would not have to review the bodies. He was the Jewish boy that Emilie had rescued from the woods after he had collapsed during the death march. He was rewarding Emilie for her kindness.

Lydia and most of the German people really did not know what had been happening in the concentration camps. Lydia thought Dachau was some kind of jail or prison and thought that it probably contained prisoners of war. She had no idea what was really happening.

After that summer day in 1945, Lydia always remembered.

Lydia and Johnny

CHAPTER 15

Pregnant — Then Married

In the long run we shape our lives and we shape ourselves.
The choices we make are ultimately our own responsibility.

Eleanor Roosevelt

During the summer of 1946, John was stationed in Munich while Lydia was working in a club and staying with a German family. When John was sent to Poland to accompany some freed Polish prisoners back to their home, Lydia decided to return home to visit her family. She was not aware that she might be pregnant. When she arrived, her mother took one look in Lydia's eyes and was immediately suspicious. She took Lydia to see a doctor, who confirmed that Lydia was pregnant. A friend of Lydia said she knew a Jewish doctor who would perform an abortion. Lydia's mother told her, "Don't you even think of doing anything about it. We will raise the child."

Lydia returned to Munich to work at the club again. When John returned from his assignment and came into the club, Lydia took one look at him and started to cry. John knew what was wrong and said not to worry. He wanted to marry her.

Getting permission to marry took so much time that John had to reenlist so he could stay in Germany. John Ross Jr. was born on January 24, 1947. John had been with Lydia in December, hoping the baby would be born then, but he had to return to his unit in January. Johnny was born at Lydia's home with a midwife in attendance. Only Lydia's father and brother were at the house, because the rest of her family was in the hospital with typhoid fever. Lydia's father discarded the afterbirth so fast that the midwife did not have time to inspect it to be sure it was complete. Some of the placenta stayed inside Lydia and made her so sick that she was in a hospital for several weeks, needing blood transfusions and intensive care. Although Lydia did not realize it then, she would be unable to have any more children.

While Lydia was in the hospital in Altötting, an ambulance came in the middle of the night with two Americans who wanted to transfer Lydia to a hospital in Austria. Lydia did not have the required pass to enter Austria, and she did not want to leave Germany. The nun at the hospital told Lydia she did not know who had requested the ambulance. Lydia thought it was suspicious and refused to leave. When John learned about it the next day, he made inquiries, but was never able to obtain any satisfactory answers. John and Lydia wondered later if there had been a conspiracy to try to smuggle someone else out of the country on that ambulance ride. When Lydia refused to leave, the two Americans left quietly.

By December 1947, over 10 months after Johnny was born, the paperwork for the marriage was finally complete. John and Lydia were married three times. On December 2 they were married by the American government and by the German government. Since they had not yet been married by the Catholic Church, Emilie insisted that John return to his unit that night. She would not permit him to sleep with Lydia until after the church service. On December 3 John and Lydia were married at Pfarrkirche Catholic Church in Neuötting. That was the anniversary date they celebrated.

Lydia's mother prepared a nice wedding dinner for them, roasting a pig with an apple in its mouth and making John's favorite dumplings. The guests were mainly siblings and some close friends. A man from Germany, Sepp, was the witness and best man. John said their 11-month-old son really enjoyed the celebration too, especially the frosting from the wedding cake.

CHAPTER 16

Typhoid Fever

Human misery must somewhere have a stop;
There is no wind that always blows a storm.

Euripides

During Lydia's pregnancy, in November 1946, most of her family came down with typhoid fever—her mother and five brothers and sisters: Luise, Carl, Anna, Elfriede, and Adolf. Only her father, brother Seigfried, and she herself escaped. Before the disease was diagnosed, Lydia received a letter from home saying how sick they were. Lydia went home to help take care of them. Fortunately, they all survived.

Typhoid fever is caused by the salmonella typhus bacteria and is transferred between humans by feces or the blood. Usually it enters the body through contaminated food, water, or drink. Lydia is not sure how her family got the disease. A canal ran past their house that connected with the Inn River. People up and down the canal dumped raw sewage into the river, not an uncommon practice in those days. Typhoid fever was rampant in Germany after the war. Some of it may have been caused by the bombing and destruction of sanitary facilities. Perhaps some was caused by the unsanitary practices of the military troops who were frequently on the move throughout the country and lacked access to sanitary facilities.

The symptoms are a high temperature (typically above 103 degrees), weakness leading to extreme fatigue, abdominal pain, diarrhea, and sometimes delirium and hallucinations. Lydia's family lost their hair.

After Lydia had been home for about 10 days and the diagnosis was confirmed, the family went to a makeshift hospital created by the German government. It was located in the old schoolhouse where Lydia had worked with the medic troops and where John had been stationed with his artillery unit.

By then Lydia was over seven months pregnant. She never returned to Munich to work, but stayed at home until the baby was born. John had a seven-day furlough at the beginning of December and came to help move the family to the hospital. They thought about quarantining John there, but because he had had shots for typhoid fever in the army, he was allowed to return to his unit. He never contracted the disease.

Some victims of the disease become "carriers" who permanently carry the bacteria in their blood stream. Even after they recover, they can infect others. Emilie became a carrier, the only one in the family who did. Emilie learned excellent sanitary habits to prevent her from infecting anyone else. Among other instructions, she was told to never sleep with her husband again or he might catch the disease. Alois was very upset, because her mother was only about 47 at the time. Lydia said he was a sexy man and kept trying to get Emilie into bed with him, but she refused and continued to sleep in the room with the girls.

COMING

TO

AMERICA

Johnny at 16 months

CHAPTER 17

April Fools' Day, 1948

The first rule of wise fiscal management is to save for a rainy day;
the second, to distinguish between light sprinkles and heavy rain.

Dian Ritter

John left Germany on a troop ship and arrived home in Minnesota on April Fools' Day in 1948. John wishes what he encountered when he arrived home would have been an April fool trick.

For three and a half years, while in Germany, John had sent a savings bond home every month. His mother, Frances, had cashed them and spent them. Perhaps she thought John would never make it home alive and would never know the difference.

When John reenlisted, he received an $800 bonus. That was a lot of money in 1946. John sent it home asking his father, Fred, to use the money to buy some pigs for the farm. Planning to marry Lydia and bring her to America, John thought pigs would be a good investment for his married life. His father never saw the money. Although Frances never admitted it, John and Fred assumed she had cashed that check too, and spent the money.

John was in predicament. His new bride and baby boy would arrive from Germany in a couple of months. There was no other choice but to have everyone move in together on the farm. He saw no way that he could establish a separate home of his own.

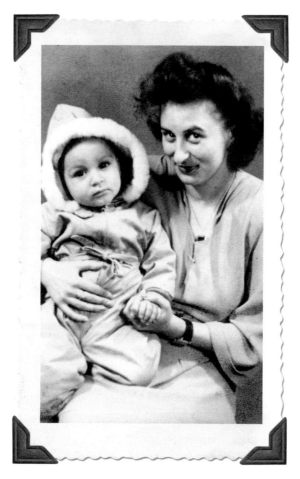

*Johnny with Lydia
at Bremerhaven, Germany, in May 1948,
before boarding the troop ship to America*

CHAPTER 18

Almost Turning Back

A child is the anchor that holds a mother to life.

Sophocles

While Lydia and young Johnny were traveling by train to the port of Bremerhaven in northern Germany to catch the troop ship to America, Johnny developed a severe ear infection. Other riders had wanted to have the windows wide open, but the noise and pressure were too much for Johnny's ears. He was admitted to the hospital in Bremerhaven.

Lydia was not permitted to stay with Johnny all of the time. Once when she came to see him, a German nurse told her that they had performed a test by taking fluid from his spine. No doubt he was being checked to ensure he did not have a disease like encephalitis or meningitis.

Lydia was upset that the test was performed without her permission and that she could not be with Johnny to comfort him. Feisty Lydia went to the doctor and said she wanted to take Johnny and go back home to Neuötting. The doctor replied, "You go ahead and go back home, Lydia, but Johnny is an American citizen and he is going to America." Lydia would not consider leaving her son. She had no choice but to continue on to America.

Lydia and Johnny boarded the troop ship, and Johnny was sent to the ship's infirmary. Lydia could visit him, but she was not allowed to take care of him. She did not get Johnny back until they landed in New York, 11 days later.

Troop ship #371 to America

CHAPTER 19

Riding the Troop Ship to America

If someone fools you once, it's his fault.
If someone fools you twice, it's your fault.

Anonymous

Lydia and Johnny shared the troop ship with about 250 soldiers, and four other war brides, three from Germany and one from France. It took 11 days to cross the ocean.

One day Lydia found a dime on the deck. A member of the military police walked by, and Lydia showed the dime to him and said, "Look what I found." He looked at it and said, "I'll trade you a bigger one for that," and showed Lydia a nickel. Lydia, not understanding the value of American money, was excited to make the swap. It was not until she told John about it later in America that she realized what had happened. Lydia's grandson, Kirk, said Lydia became very discerning about the value of money when she lived in America. He remembers one day when they were aboard a train, and Lydia asked the porter for some gum. He brought a package and charged 25 cents. Lydia looked at the package and saw that the label was marked 20 cents. Lydia went straight to the porter and demanded a nickel back. No one could explain to her that there might be an extra charge for "delivering" the gum. Rather than argue, the porter gave a nickel back to Lydia.

On the troop ship, Lydia had no money with her. She would have been unable to use any German money if she had had any. Since the meals were free, she really did not need any money on the ship.

Young Johnny was riding in the infirmary with his ear infection. Lydia was sad that she could not be with him the whole time, but she did visit him when she could.

The troop ship landed in New York City in the early evening. No one was allowed to disembark until the next morning. Lydia said that the city lights awed her and that it was mesmerizing to look at the huge city from the ship and watch the night shine brightly from the lights.

The next morning, an enthusiastic and energized Lydia was the first to disembark. She was given Johnny Jr. as she left the ship.

CHAPTER 20

Traveling from New York to Minnesota

Love doesn't make the world go round —
Love is what makes the ride worthwhile.

Franklin P. Jones

Landing in New York was both frightening and exciting for Lydia. She spoke only broken English in a strange new country. Johnny did not walk and tiny Lydia had to carry him wherever they went. He was a big boy for 16 months.

The first task for Lydia was to take Johnny to the Army doctor. Johnny had to be discharged like the American citizen he was. When Lydia reached the doctor, he said, "Oh, if it isn't Johnny Ross. He was my last patient in Germany." It was the same doctor who had told Lydia that she could go back to Bavaria if she wanted but that Johnny was going to America because he was an American citizen.

The Red Cross gave Lydia $10 for the trip to Minnesota. Lydia and Johnny boarded a train to Chicago. On the way to Chicago, Lydia decided to order a meal on the train. They had a menu, but she could not read it. She pointed to something and said that was what she would have. When it came, it was a huge round steak. It cost $7 which left only $3 for the rest of the trip. Lydia disliked the meat and ate none of it. She did enjoy all of the trimmings and other food that came with the meal. It was the only meal Lydia ate on the train. Her other $3 bought milk for Johnny. Except for three pennies, she had no money left when she arrived in Chicago.

In Chicago, Lydia had to change trains and stations. Still unfamiliar with the currency, she found a taxi driver and showed him her three pennies. He shook his head. The Red Cross took her and Johnny to the other train station. Lydia said the Red Cross was very helpful in their journey across America. The Red Cross also paid for the tickets for her and Johnny to take the train to Mankato.

When Lydia boarded the 400 train to Mankato, her money was gone. Young Johnny was hungry and crying. A man from Mankato was on the train, and when Lydia explained why Johnny was crying, he took Johnny's bottle and brought it back full, along with some sandwiches for Lydia.

The train arrived in Mankato at midnight. The man who bought the food told Lydia that he would take Lydia and Johnny the 20 miles to Elysian if no one met them.

John was anxiously waiting at the station to greet his wife and son. His Jeep was in poor condition, so neighbor Harvey Call drove John, his mother, and his father to the station. Lydia thought Harvey must be the chauffeur. To exchange cars, they first went to Harvey's farmhouse which was about a mile from the Ross farm. When they arrived, Harvey's wife, Ella, had lunch ready for them. Lydia thought she was the maid. Lydia said that it was a good lunch, but that she was not very hungry. When she realized that she was not in the Ross house and that they had to travel further, she just wanted to get to her new home after the long trip. After lunch they drove home in John's Jeep. It was May 24, 1948.

WORKING YEARS

IN

AMERICA

Grandpa Ross giving Johnny a piggyback ride
under the watchful eye of Lydia

CHAPTER 21

The American Dream — Shattered and Rebuilt

The U.S. Constitution does not guarantee happiness,
only the pursuit of it.
You have to catch up with it yourself.

Benjamin Franklin

As Lydia sailed across the ocean to America, she wondered what she would find in this new land full of hope and promise. She dreamed of a wonderful and happy life in the land of opportunity. Would Elysian be anything like Elysian Fields, the place in Greek mythology that was full of song, joy, and sunshine, where people danced in the flowers and meadows? What she found was a mother-in-law who had spent John's savings, leaving them with no option but to move into the family home. What was home like? It had:

- NO running water
- NO electricity, except for one small light that John had managed to wire
- NO plumbing
- NO phone
- NO sheets on the mattresses that they used for beds
- NO privacy from a meddling mother-in-law

It was a very old house. Lydia said she did not have much in Germany either, but that at least her family took pride in what they had and kept it clean and in good repair.

The one bright spot was that young Johnny Jr. loved his grandpa and took to him right away. Perhaps Fred looked a little like the grandfather Johnny loved and left behind in Germany. It took a little while for Johnny Jr. to get reacquainted with his father. Fred was good to Lydia and tried to help her adjust to the new land.

Lydia had difficulty adjusting. She was very sad, and getting sadder. After two years at the farm, Lydia knew what she needed to do for self-preservation. She walked the mile with young Johnny to her neighbor, Ella Call. Lydia and Ella had become good friends, and Lydia walked there almost every day. She asked Ella to take her to the bank in town. Lydia told the banker that she had to get out of that farmhouse. Was there any way she could borrow some money?

Lydia was a German citizen without a job and still spoke only broken English. Her feisty determination must have been convincing. Everybody knows everyone in a small town. The compassionate banker said there was an old house for sale in town that he would sell to Lydia for $1,000. She would need to put $300 down. The loan would have to be in Lydia's name only and not John's. John's family had a poor reputation for handling money.

That night Lydia told her husband about the deal. She said she had to move whether or not John would come with her. John, himself being disillusioned with life on the farm, wanted to be with her and agreed to move.

John asked his father for money for the down payment. John had worked at the farm for two years and had not received any wages. Frances would drive to town to get the check for the cream that was sold, and no one ever knew what became of the money. She probably bought some groceries, but there should have been money left. Occasionally Fred would give John a dollar to take

Lydia to the movies or to a dance. When John came home, the family asked him to take out a $10,000 loan to buy machinery and livestock for the farm. Lydia had to sign the loan, too, and did not really know what she was signing because she could not read English. Fred agreed to give John the $300 for the down payment. It was only a fraction of what was really owed to John.

Lydia was thrilled. She said that although the house was not much – just one big room on the first floor with a full basement underneath – it was everything to her. It was her emancipation from a horrible living situation. Neighbors and people in town gave her furniture. John found a job in the local hatchery where chickens were hatched and cleaned. He was paid $1 an hour. He worked there a year before finding a better paying job at Al's Construction Co., where he worked another year. He then worked on construction on Highway 13. He kept seeking better jobs and was finally hired by Hubbard Sunshine Feeds in Mankato, 20 miles away. He worked there 37 years until retiring at age 60. In those days, flour was often sold in 50-pound cotton print flour sacks. Forerunners of the recycling movement, the sacks were then used to make dresses, aprons, pillowcases, sheets, and anything that could be sewed from cotton. John brought some sacks home from the plant, and they made curtains for the house from them.

After moving into the new house, Lydia started working in a restaurant owned by Hattie Studer. Lydia's main job was to wait on people. She still spoke little English. She could not write anything down, so she had to memorize the orders. She said she "got along OK." She was able to take young Johnny to work with her. Her salary included free meals for the family. Hattie was kind to her. Things began looking up. The house payments were $25 a month. John and Lydia paid extra on the house and had it paid in full in a little over a year.

The house began as 12 feet by 20 feet. While John and Lydia owned the home, John added two bedrooms, which he moved in from his farmhouse and one living room moved from a friend's house. It takes a handy man to move rooms and attach them to another house.

Lydia dressed Johnny in a white outfit.
Grandpa Ross gave some tools to Johnny and let
him play. Notice the grease on his face and clothes.

CHAPTER 22

Learning to Cook

The way to a man's heart is through his stomach.

Anonymous

Every new bride has tales of learning to cook. An incident John likes to recall happened shortly after Lydia arrived in America. John's family killed a chicken on the farm and put it on the kitchen table for Lydia to cook while they left to go to Mankato. Although Lydia had cooked chicken before, she had never prepared one right off the farm. She had to remove the feathers, clean out the inside, cut it into serving pieces, and get it ready to fry. She said she wore her good cotton gloves to clean out the inside. Then she dumped the gloves and everything she removed from the chicken into the outhouse. When the family sat down to eat, Fred took his favorite piece, the gizzard, a tough organ in birds whose function is to receive the food from the stomach and grind it up fine for digestion. Fred took one bite and got a mouthful of gravel and corn. Lydia did not know that a gizzard needs to be cut in half so the inside can be cleaned out before cooking. John said the rest of the chicken tasted good. Lydia must have learned her lesson well. While she was working at the Birdseye canning factory several years later, the company made a video of her preparing and cutting up a chicken, which was used to train new employees.

Lydia had an excellent reputation for her cooking. She especially loved making dishes that she had learned to make in Germany. She did not have to cook much at home in Germany because she always had a job, and her mother had the food ready when she returned from work. But she did have some jobs that required cooking, and she did help her mother sometimes and learned to cook German specialties. John loved her dumplings and sauerkraut dishes. Lydia was an excellent gardener and one of her favorite treats to share with the neighbors was German radish sandwiches. She buttered thin slices of German sourdough rye bread and spread salted slices of white German radishes on top. The radishes grow long and large and can be sliced into circular pieces. It is delicious. It may have been something Lydia's family learned to eat during the Depression and during the war when food and money was scarce in Germany. Lydia got radish seed from Germany from her niece and nephew and bought German sourdough bread. Other neighbors recall the succulent sliced salted kohlrabies straight from her garden.

Another of Lydia's specialties was German potato salad. She brought it to most of the potluck dinners frequently held at the American Legion club in Elysian and other places. People would look for her special dish and be disappointed if she happened to miss the event or not bring the treat. She never really measured ingredients so it was impossible to get an exact recipe. But an adventurous person could try this recipe which Lydia shared.

Good luck! It may not ever taste exactly like Lydia's, but it might come close.

Recipe from the kitchen of Lydia

German Potato Salad

Boil a pot full of potatoes with the jackets on.
Peel and slice while still warm.
Fry some slices of bacon until crisp, along with some onions.
Crumble the bacon.
Mix together oil, vinegar, and sugar, to taste.
Mix everything together along with some raw onions.
Heat in a crock pot. Serve warm.

CHAPTER 23

Working at the Canning Factory

Take your work seriously, but yourself lightly.

C. W. Metcalf

Lydia had been working at the restaurant in Elysian for about six months when some friends asked her if she would like to ride with them to work at the Birdseye canning factory in Waseca, about 13 miles from Elysian. The pay was 75 cents an hour. Lydia thought that sounded good. It would have taken almost four days to earn that much money at Lydia's first job in Munich.

Lydia said she learned a lot of English while working at the canning factory. Some of it was good, and some of it was not so good. Some of it she could not trust. One day some of her friends told her that a plane high in the sky was a bird. When she told John about the new word she learned that day, he corrected her. She realized that they had played a joke on her. Several days later they asked her about a small scar the size of a dime that was on her neck. Lydia told them it happened when she was shot by the Americans because she would not give in to them. That was where the bullet had hit her, she jokingly said. John and Lydia spoke German in their home when Lydia first came to America, but Lydia kept working at learning English.

Lydia was always full of fun and a delight to be around. One prank she enjoyed at work was to slide down the banister at the end of the corn pack. The corn was processed on the second floor, and a long curving banister on the stairs went from the first floor to the second. As a way of celebrating the end of the corn season, Lydia and a couple friends slid down the banister. The second year they did it, the supervisor just shrugged and said, "Don't you girls ever grow up?"

Lydia worked there for two years. The plant slowed down after the harvest each year. As a new employee, Lydia was laid off during the winter months. After the second season, she decided to look elsewhere for year-round work.

Lydia and Johnny after move to Elysian

CHAPTER 24

Sewing Piece Work at Munsingwear

There is a kind of victory in good work, no matter how humble.

Jack Kemp

After the canning factory closed for the season, Lydia found work in a Munsingwear plant in Montgomery. Munsingwear was a brand of underwear and t-shirts. Her main job was to sew the elastic on undershorts. She was paid by the number of pieces she sewed. Lydia worked quickly and said she "made good money" at the job.

One day Lydia's supervisor brought a new sewing machine to her. He wanted to see how many pieces she could sew in a certain amount of time. Lydia knew they were setting a new standard for her, so she sewed at a leisurely pace. The supervisor said, "Lydia, you can sew faster than that." Lydia replied, "Just because you have a new machine with a new motor in it does not mean that you can put a new motor in me."

The supervisor did not like Lydia's response. She was called into the office to talk with the management. A union representative in the office told Lydia she should cooperate with the study. Lydia asked him who he was working for, the management or her.

After the study was over, Lydia again worked quickly and sewed much faster than most of the other workers. Lydia worked at the factory for about 10 years. The workers then went on strike, and the factory never reopened after the strike.

husband John Sr.

son Johnny Jr.

grandson Kirk

*The Ross men:
husband John Sr.,
son Johnny Jr.,
and grandson Kirk
The resemblance is striking.*

CHAPTER 25

Tragedy Strikes

Into each life, some rain must fall.

Henry Wadsworth Longfellow

John's family enjoyed the outdoors, especially hunting and fishing. In the fall of 1953, Fred went to Hill City with John and some friends to hunt deer. Fred was accidentally shot by a friend. John said he walked about 90 feet before he dropped. John drove him to a hospital, but he died on the way. The bullet had gone through his heart as it passed through his body. He was 62 years old.

It was a sad day for the Ross family. Little Johnny Jr. was six years old. Lydia told him about the accident after he returned home from school. It was a great shock for everyone.

A few days after the funeral, Frances came with her lawyer to see John. She needed cash and wanted to sell the Jeep. The lawyer had some papers for John to sign. He said they would give Frances permission to sell the Jeep. The lawyer pointed to the dotted line. John signed the papers, as did his only brother and only sister.

Some time after they had all signed the papers, they inquired about the inheritance and estate, and were informed that they had signed off not only on the Jeep, but also on the entire estate. Frances shared some of the money with the only daughter. John received only a small canvas fishing boat.

After Frances had spent the inheritance, she asked John and Lydia if she could move into their home so they could take care of her. Once again feisty Lydia needed to practice self-preservation and she responded the only way she could. Regardless, John and Lydia were both working full time and would not have been home to take care of her. Frances had by then suffered a stroke and was in a wheelchair. She could not take care of herself, so she moved into a nursing home.

John said that he thinks his mother did not like Lydia very much because she never quite believed that Johnny Jr. was John's son. She thought maybe Lydia had set a trap so she could come to America. One look at Johnny Jr., as well as his son Kirk, leaves no doubt that they are the son and grandson of John Sr.

Frances died in 1979 at the age of 82. It was 26 years after her husband, Fred, died in a hunting accident.

Johnny Jr., age 9 with Lydia,
passport picture, 1956

CHAPTER 26

First Trip Back to Germany

You cannot prevent the birds of sorrow from flying over your head,
but you can prevent them from building nests in your hair.

Dian Ritter

It was with bittersweet emotion that Lydia and young Johnny boarded a plane to Germany in November 1956. Lydia had not been back to her homeland or seen her family since she had left in 1948. Johnny was 16 months old then and was now nine.

Lydia had received a letter from Emilie saying that Alois was dying of cancer. Although money was tight, John knew Lydia needed to return to say her goodbyes.

Lydia went to her favorite banker in Elysian, Raoul La France, to see if she could borrow money for the trip. Lydia was receiving a good salary from the Munsingwear factory, and again the banker loaned the money to Lydia only. John said Lydia could always get money out of the banker when she needed it because she had a reputation for working hard to pay it back. John said he could not get even a plug nickel because of his family's reputation.

Lydia's father enjoyed the visit. When they arrived, he was well enough to take Johnny with him on excursions. A favorite place was beer joints, where Johnny could get a treat. They loved to play cards together, although Alois said Johnny liked to win too much and cheated. Johnny was always Grandpa's boy when he was a baby, and the bond continued during that visit. When Johnny returned from Germany after three months, he was speaking perfect German.

While in Germany, Lydia happened to meet a former boyfriend in town. This was Sepp, who had been the best man at her wedding. She first had met him when they were both working at the medic unit. He had been a prisoner of war in England and was brought to work at the unit. He brought dirty clothes back and forth to the laundry where Emilie worked near their house. He told Lydia that if she did not like it in America, she could come home to Germany and he would marry her. Lydia was not tempted. Her friend eventually married a woman who had 10 children.

Lydia and Johnny returned to Minnesota in January. John Sr. said it had been the loneliest and longest three months of his life. Lydia's father died a month later.

Lydia in Germany with her parents,
Emilie and Alois Weber, and son Johnny
December 1956

CHAPTER 27

Thrilled to Be
an American Citizen

There ain't no doubt I love this land.
God bless the USA!

Lee Greenwood

There was a required seven-year wait to become an American citizen. During that time, Lydia learned as much English, and as much about America, as she could. She had to go to St. Paul to take the test.

The tests were given orally, which was easier for Lydia than trying to read and write English. The candidates were called into the examining room individually. She did not pass the first time. She tried again a week later and was successful! She remembered only one question: "If the president should die, who would become president?" The answer was Nixon. The year was 1955.

She needed two witnesses. She used her former neighbor on the farm, Ella Call, and her good friend Mildred Roemhildt.

Dwight D. Eisenhower was now the president of the United States. The next year, 1956, was the first time Lydia was eligible to vote for president. She asked John for advice on who should receive her vote. John said she had to decide for herself. Dwight D. Eisenhower was running for re-election. She thought he had done a good job as commander of the Allied forces in Europe, so she voted for him. On the way home, John asked her who did receive her vote. When she told him, he said, "Well, that killed my vote."

Lydia took pride in voting and was serious about her responsibilities as a citizen. She was an active member of the American Legion Auxiliary, and she tried to learn all she could about candidates and issues.

In retirement, one of John and Lydia's favorite pastimes was to attend the Elysian City Council meetings. Lydia spoke her mind on issues whether or not she was recognized from the floor. Most town officials delighted in her participation and were pleased that she took such an interest in the affairs of the city.

Lydia wanted everyone to know that she was very happy she came to the United States. She believed this is the best country in the world!

Bavaria, taken on a trip back to Germany

CHAPTER 28

Proud to Be from Bavaria

That which we have been makes us what we are.

Anonymous

There was no question about it: Lydia was proud to be from Bavaria, located in the southeast corner of Germany. It is the largest state in Germany and comprises 27,239 square miles. The population is 12,532,000. Munich is the capital. Bavarians are proud of their heritage and continue to foster their culture. When asked where they are from, the answer is usually Bavaria rather than Germany.

The Bavarian flag flew underneath the American flag on the pole located on the lake side of Lydia's home. Lydia much preferred the Bavarian flag to the German flag, as do most Bavarians. She was especially proud that the current pope, Benedict XVI, was born in Marktl am Inn, on the Inn River, just a mile and a half from Lydia's hometown. He is one and a half years younger than Lydia. When Lydia heard that Cardinal Joseph Ratzinger was named Pope in 2005, she wondered if she may have met or even dated him. However, he left the city of his birth when he was two years old. He moved to nearby Traunstein and claims that area of Bavaria as his childhood home. Lydia proudly displayed his picture in her house.

As one approaches Lydia and John's house, there is a sign beside the garage door that reads "Parking for Germans only." Inside the home are many dishes and other memorabilia from Germany. A magnet on the refrigerator says, "You can always tell a German, but you can't tell him much!"

Flowers were as prevalent at Lydia's house as they are in Bavaria. She had the proverbial green thumb and had an array of flowers in her garden strategically planted to bloom throughout the spring, summer, and fall. In Minnesota, flowers take a rest during the winter months. She also had a flourishing vegetable garden.

Once, Lydia's neighbor, Dave Thayer, was attempting to train a new German shorthair dog to sit on command. The dog was not responding to his verbal command, "Sit." Lydia saw this, came over to Dave, and said to the dog authoritatively, "Sitzen." The dog immediately sat. Lydia said, "This is a German dog and responds only to German commands." Of course, the dog had never lived in Germany and would not recognize the German language, but Lydia was able to get him to sit by speaking German – if not only because of her commanding voice. Dave has trained many dogs and is still amazed at how the dog responded to Lydia.

Bavarians are known for their sociability and Lydia was no exception. She was a wonderful neighbor whose coffee pot was always on. Coffee was usually accompanied with some homemade cookies or dessert.

John loves the German culture and loved his German war bride. He has his own lederhosen, which he will proudly show to you. Lydia enjoyed saying in jest, "John came over to Germany to fight the Germans, and he is still fighting the Germans."

CHAPTER 29

Living on Lake Francis

He is happiest, be he king or peasant, who finds peace in his home.

Johann von Goethe

After living for 12 years in their house that began as one room, Lydia began yearning for something newer and larger. Both she and John had steady jobs, and it seemed they could afford a better house. Lydia heard about a home for sale about half a mile outside Elysian on the north shore of Lake Francis. Two stories and three bedrooms, it was perfect for John and Lydia. The lot was almost level to a wonderfully clear lake with good fishing. The lake was 3 miles long and 60 feet deep at the deepest points. It was spring-fed and remained clear. The view was breathtaking.

John and Lydia decided to make an offer. Once again Lydia went to her favorite banker and obtained the required loan. This time John's name was on the loan, too. By now they both had an excellent reputation for honesty and for handling money well. One example happened one Monday morning when they went to pick up some meat from their foot locker at John Nusbaum's grocery store and meat market. They opened the foot locker and saw a big brown paper bag full of money. They showed it to John Nusbaum, and he said, "Oh, we hide our money in your locker over the weekend until we can get to the bank on Monday, because we know if you find it you will be honest and tell us." In 1962 John and Lydia moved to their home on the lake, where they lived for about 46 years until health problems forced Lydia to join John in a nursing home in 2008.

Lydia with grandchildren Christine and Kirk

The lake home was perfect for the things John and Lydia enjoyed. There was excellent fishing in both summer and winter. Their ice house in later years was equipped with a television, a CB radio, a heater, and benches.

Lydia canned much of her garden produce, like pickled beets and tomatoes. Her produce was often the first in the area to ripen and she had the most abundant harvest. When Lydia moved to a nursing home, her neighbor asked permission to use the garden plot. With all the rabbits, bugs, and weeds, the neighbor could not reap the harvest that Lydia had. That magical plot had lost the master's touch.

John and Lydia had a deck on the second floor of their home and a patio on the ground level. The sunsets were beautiful. They kept a birdhouse for martins in the yard that helped control the mosquitoes.

They had lots of company at the lake. Many people enjoyed the boating, fishing, swimming, and water skiing. It was especially busy the first year they had the house. One weekend they left so they would not have company, but when they returned there were people waiting. It always seemed as if the company came in the summer after the dock, lift, and boat were in the water and disappeared in the fall before it was time to remove them from the water.

Feeding bread crumbs to the fish, 1977

After Lydia stopped fishing, the whole lake became her fishbowl. She fed the fish bread crumbs from her dock. No one was allowed to fish from that dock. When Lydia stepped onto the dock, one could see the fish gathering for their feast of bread crumbs. Her grandchildren, great-grandchildren, and many of the neighbors enjoyed the same experience of feeding the fish.

John was 38 when they bought the home. He wanted to have it paid by the time he was 50. So they made extra payments when they could afford it, and the home was paid in full within 12 years by John's 50th birthday.

Home on Lake Francis

CHAPTER 30

An Avid High School Sports Fan

Some people are like buttons, always popping off.

Dian Ritter

John Jr. was an excellent athlete and Lydia was his biggest fan. She never missed a game. Lydia became emotional about all the games. Johnny says that although she never understood much about the rules, she knew when officials made a call against her favorite team.

The fall sport was football. One night the Waterville High School team for which Johnny played, was given a five-yard penalty. (Waterville, six miles from Elysian, was the area's high school.) Lydia marched onto the playing field to object. The referee gave the team an additional 10-yard penalty before she was ushered off the field.

During basketball season, John Sr. would not sit with Lydia. He sat on the highest row away from the playing floor, while she sat in the front row and never hesitated to speak her mind. Once when she was unhappy about a call, she went up to the referee, who was clad in the traditional black and white stripes and told him, "That shirt suits you just fine. You should be in Sing Sing for the call you just made."

In the spring, John Jr. went out for track. He held the school's pole-vaulting record for over 20 years. His record was 11 feet.

Lydia continued to attend high school sports events with John for years after their son graduated. She eventually cheered for her granddaughter, Christine, who played basketball. Christine also had a beautiful singing voice, and Lydia enjoyed her concerts. Grandson Kirk was an artist. Lydia was proud to see his drawings around the school and town. He redesigned the mascot Buccaneer that appeared on the school programs, and he designed road signs and memorabilia for special celebrations.

Lydia and John at their
25th wedding anniversary celebration

CHAPTER 31

Surviving Yet Again

*Life is not always what one wants it to be,
but to make the best of it as it is, is the only way of being happy.*

Jennie Jerome Churchill

Lydia seemed to be like the cat with nine lives. She was in several death-defying situations, one of them a car accident in St. Paul.

One fall while Lydia was working at Munsingwear, John and Johnny went deer hunting in northern Minnesota. Lydia's friend Patty Rust asked her if she would like to ride along with her and another friend, Pat Quiram, to take Patty's son back to college in the Twin Cities. Before they could leave St. Paul, a severe winter storm developed. It was icy, and the roads became very slippery. While Patty was driving on an overpass, the car slid off the road onto the pavement below. It flipped and spun around. Lydia suffered a broken back, ribs, shoulder, and nose.

Lydia was taken to Ramsey County Hospital in St. Paul. After she had been there about a week, she started growing impatient because she was not permitted to get out of bed to go to the bathroom. John was visiting when Lydia asked the doctor if she could get out of bed to use the bathroom or a commode. The doctor refused, and John asked why. He answered forcefully, "Do you really want your wife to get up with a broken back?" John did not like his response or his tone, so the next day he requested an ambulance to take Lydia home to the hospital in Mankato.

When Pat Quiram and Lydia were in the emergency room immediately following the accident, the nurses asked Pat if Lydia's nose looked crooked. Pat answered, "No, it always looks like that." So nothing was done with the broken nose, and it healed crooked. Just before she was discharged from the hospital in St. Paul, her nose was rebroken and set again so it could heal straight. She had bandages covering her face when she arrived in Mankato. Her doctor thought she looked like a ghost and removed most of them. Lydia was in the hospital from six to eight weeks and came home just before Christmas. She could not return to work for a year. Once again she had narrowly escaped death.

John and Lydia on their dock, 1975

CHAPTER 32

Working Years at E F Johnson

Giving your best today is the recipe for a better tomorrow.

Dian Ritter

After the Munsingwear plant closed, Lydia found work on the assembly line at E F Johnson in Waseca. The factory made wireless communication devices like handheld radios, ham radios, police radios, two-way radios, and all the component parts. Lydia worked on the assembly line for circuit boards for 22 years, from 1964 until 1986. During her last seven years, Bob Tetzloff was in charge of Lydia's area. He said that Lydia was a hard worker and always good-natured. If he ever needed to tell her something he spoke to her in German. Shirley Roemhildt, her immediate line supervisor during most of the 22 years, said there was only one problem with Lydia: She could work fast with her hands, but she talked as fast as she worked. Her voice was loud and her accent thick, and the other girls on the line often stopped working to listen carefully so they could understand her. Both Bob and Shirley had to ask Lydia to limit her talking. People who worked at the plant when Lydia was there said that everyone knew and loved Lydia and that her presence was unmistakable.

Shirley became good friends with Lydia. Before long, three couples were meeting every Saturday night to play cards: John and Lydia Ross, Mel and Shirley Roemhildt, and Les and Ardelle Rients. The usual card game was six-handed 500, but they also played euchre. The women played against the men. Lydia thoroughly enjoyed many different games of cards. It was a wonderful way to have an inexpensive evening of fun in a time when there was little money for entertainment.

Shirley recalls that once when she and Mel were visiting John and Lydia at their lake home, they went swimming. Shirley could float, but Lydia did not know how to swim. Shirley offered to teach Lydia to float by holding out her arms and asking Lydia to lie back on top of them. While Lydia was lying on top of Shirley's arms, she let go. Down Lydia went to the bottom. Shirley said, "By the time I pulled Lydia back above the water, you can imagine what she said to me." Lydia never again allowed Shirley to play swimming instructor, nor did she learn to swim.

Technology had begun changing by 1986, and communication devices were becoming more sophisticated. Business at E F Johnson was declining, and workers were laid off. Although Lydia had seniority and probably could have worked longer, she decided it was time to retire. John had already retired. She retired at the age of 61.

Lydia's retirement from E F Johnson, 1986

Young Johnny with neighbor Carol Call
a few years after arriving in America

FUN MEMORIES

FROM

FRIENDS AND FAMILY

John, Lydia, and neighbor Betty Haus
Boarding the elevator for the ride to the top of
the Gateway Arch, St. Louis

CHAPTER 33

Notes from Neighbors

No one is rich enough to do without a neighbor.

Harold Helfer

Lydia was very sociable and had many friends. It seems like everyone in town has a cute story to share about her. A few were censored and a few are included.

Prose from Pat

Pat Quiram knew Lydia almost since the day she arrived in Elysian. A thank-you letter had arrived from Germany for some clothes that had been donated through Josco's. It was written in German and needed to be translated. Pat's family had heard of Lydia, and they asked her for help. Lydia could read the letter, and with John's help she translated it.

Pat spoke to Darlene Simons Adams and Carol Call Warweg. Together they shared the following stories:

When Lydia first arrived from Germany, Ella Call held a personal wedding shower for her. Twenty-six women attended and Lydia received seven alluring negligees. When John came to take her home after the shower, Lydia proudly showed them to him and said, "Look John, we can go dancing." Lydia thought they were ballroom gowns.

Soon after Lydia came to America, she purchased a colorful pair of argyle socks. She thought they looked great with a pair of high heels that she had. (Fashions were probably different in

Germany.) Finally her friends told her they would not go with her to Mankato if she continued wearing the socks with the heels.

Ella and her daughter, Carol, took Lydia to Holton's Cafeteria in Mankato for lunch. Lydia had never eaten in a cafeteria and thought she could take all the food she wanted for one price, so she piled her tray high with food. When she reached the check-out line, the bill was $9 -- a lot of money when a hamburger and malt at Hattie's in Elysian could be had for 35 cents. She re-traced her steps and put back all the food that she could. Carol and Ella helped her pay for the rest of the food.

Lydia struggled to learn English. She took no formal classes and learned gradually from others and through experiences. Pat Quiram says Lydia once fed Ex-lax to Johnny because she thought it was candy.

Darlene Simons and Carol Call both recall Lydia's generosity at their weddings. So they could wear "something borrowed," Lydia let them wear one of her rings.

Stories from the Shafts

Stewart and Shirley Shaft purchased their lake cabin on the west side of John and Lydia's house in 1970. During the summer months, they lived there with their six children until 1976. Lydia's first thought when she heard that a family with six kids was moving next door was "There goes our peace and quiet." But it did not take long before they were one happy family. Shirley said John and Lydia were the best neighbors ever. Only one thing concerned Shirley: Lydia's frequent use of colorful language. Shirley told Lydia that her children were young, and if Lydia wanted to use those words, perhaps she could say them in German so the children would not understand. Lydia tried hard, but often slipped. When she did, she clasped her hand over her mouth and looked at Shirley. Shirley hugged her, thanked her, and encouraged her to keep trying.

All the Shafts adored John and Lydia. There was not a thing the Rosses would not do for the Shafts. They especially liked it when Lydia shared the special German radishes from her garden. Lydia smuggled the seeds out of Germany on one of her trips back to her home land. This was of course illegal, but Lydia hid them in her bra knowing the customs authorities were not about to search there. Lydia was greatly endowed in the bust area and it was easy for her to hide the seeds. Lydia had a special utensil that she stuck in the top of the large peeled radish and twisted it around to make a spiral. The spiraled radish was placed on a plate and salted. It was delicious.

In the summer, John and Lydia enjoyed a bottle of beer on the deck after work. The Shaft kids got their first taste of beer from them. The Shafts had no liquor in their house, and the children were curious about the taste. Lydia could not resist satisfying their curiosity. German children first tasted beer when they were very young.

Once when Stewart was gone, a strong storm developed. Shirley was alone with the kids. The Shafts owned an airplane that was parked in the front yard next to the lake. John helped Shirley check to see if the plane was fastened securely. The wind blew so hard that it covered the docks and pontoons of the plane with seaweed. Some of the docks were pulled from their moorings. There was a lot of cleanup to be done the next day.

John and Lydia were especially helpful when young Marty Shaft had tubes put in his ears and had to stay out of the water for an entire summer. Of all the children in the family, he was the "fish." He learned to swim early and was fearless when it came to water activities. It was hard to keep him out of the water. Lydia was very helpful in keeping him occupied onshore, so that he would stay on land.

Shirley recalls hearing about a New Year's Eve party at the Corner Bar in Elysian that John and Lydia attended, along with many other people from Elysian. Lydia loved to party and have a good time. With the aid of some spirits, she started dancing wildly on top of one of the tables. John decided there had been enough partying for one night and he took her home.

The Shaft children also contributed comments about Lydia. The stories from Shari, Stew II, Scot, and Marc are included here and the memories from Mike follow separately.

Shari Shaft Sneary, the youngest Shaft and the only girl with five older brothers, says she did not enjoy the lake activities as much as things that were done on land. Summers meant spending time at their lake cabin with some very special people: John and Lydia and their grandchildren, Kirk and Christine. Shari said they always made you feel welcome no matter how young you were. The door was always open to the Shaft kids. Shari said no one could hug like Lydia—her hugs stayed with you the rest of the day! There were also many interesting conversations and lots of yummy treats in Lydia's kitchen.

Stew II remembers Lydia as a bubbly personality wrapped in a cute little package. He pictures her "fussing in her garden" and says she was a delightful, energetic, earthy, good-humored woman with a wonderfully thick German accent, whose infectious laugh could be heard around the lake.

Scot remembers it was rumored that Lydia always went skinny-dipping on her birthday. The Shaft boys could see that Lydia was well-endowed, and they wanted to stay awake to sneak a peek. Scot said he never knew if the story were true, because the boys were always either fast asleep, or were not permitted to sneak out of their bedrooms that late at night. Scot also recalls Lydia's delicious onion sandwiches. He thought he would never eat bullhead until Lydia cooked them, and then he thought they were delicious. Scot also remembers that although Lydia's thick German accent could make it difficult to understand her, her English swear words were loud and clear.

Marc says he once took his slingshot and filled his pockets with rocks to see what he could hit around the cabin. He first went into the wooded swamp area across the road, but it seemed to take too much energy to sneak around in the bug-infested woods in the hopes of finding the rare squirrel or rabbit. He thought there had to be an easier target somewhere -- and it was the purple martin hotel-shaped birdhouse in front of John and Lydia's house. Flocks of birds regularly circled and landed, especially at sunset when the insects, their major food source, buzzed around. Marc said Lydia caught him dead to rights with no out, slingshot and rocks in hand. Lydia read him the riot act in her thick accent. Marc said he understood every word. No purple martins were ever harmed.

Lydia also could come to Marc's aid. Once when Stew II was upset over losing a water game the brothers were playing, he picked up a paddle from a water toy and hurled it like a javelin. It struck Marc above the right eye, and blood shot out. Lydia helped administer direct pressure and first aid before the trip to the doctor for the required stitches.

Memories from Mike

Michael Shaft has special memories of Lydia involving her garden:

If there were one recurring memory I have of Lydia Ross, it is her dedication to her garden. Mornings and evenings would often find her doing all the things good gardeners do: prepping the soil (usually by hand), planting, watering, weeding, and in general giving it the love it needed to produce.

The garden was her slice of heaven, and no one defended it more fiercely than Lydia. Whether it were rabbits, neighbor dogs, birds, pests or any other threat, no one, and I mean no one was allowed to mess with Lydia's personal "patch" of happiness.

I learned a number of German phrases when I was around her and her gardening, and although I asked, I was never given the English translation. The passion and furor with which those words were directed at weeds and garden pests made me intuitively understand that they might just be bad words.

All of this leads up to a special memory — one that involves my brothers and I running around doing what boys do, when I happened to run right through the middle of Lydia's garden. I instantly knew I was in no man's land, and fear consumed me. I felt like Peter Rabbit with Lydia as Mr. McGregor. I anticipated the tongue-lashing, then having my parents called in on my violation of sacred territory, along with the giggles and teasing I knew my brothers would unleash.

This is where a great lesson was learned. Instead of an instant explosion of anger, Lydia asked me to come inside the house and sit down at the dinner table. I remember wondering what tortures awaited. Instead, Lydia was busy preparing a sandwich on the counter. She came over, looked at me and told me to eat it. She had my complete attention and I complied. There was an explosion of taste like nothing I had ever experienced before. After devouring the sandwich, I asked her, "What was that?" She told me it was a white German radish sandwich with mayo! I could not believe it—a vegetable? Are you kidding me? I was raised on moose meat and potatoes. I did not have time for veggies!

But here is the kicker: Lydia said, "If you want more of those sandwiches, you have to be careful not to run through the garden." Isn't that a great teaching example? What patience! And the best part of the story is that I never again did anything to mess with Lydia's garden. And nor did I let anybody or anything else!

Just wanted to tell everyone that besides her feisty spirit, Lydia had a gentle side, too!

Whimsical Winner from Weber

Ice fishing contests have been held on Lake Francis during February for most of the years that John and Lydia lived on the lake. The Community Club in Elysian was the first group to host the contests as a fund raiser. The American Legion in town has been the host for the past twenty years. The event is typically held very close to the front of John and Lydia's home and is attended by hundreds of people. In addition to the big prizes, local merchants from the surrounding area donate prizes that are distributed at the contest at a rate of about one every 30 seconds. People need to be present to win.

As an auctioneer, Herb Weber is the perfect person to emcee the awarding of the prizes each year. Lydia frequently complained to him that she sold many tickets to her co-workers at E F Johnson and never won a prize. One year Herb and a friend decided to play a trick on Lydia. About halfway through the contest, Herb announced into the microphone, "Lydia Ross is our next winner. Please report to the winner's table to claim your prize." Lydia was very excited. When she arrived at the table, Herb asked her to open the envelope and read the prize into the microphone. She read, "This coupon is good for one free enema at the Waterville Clinic."

Herb says that he can still hear the "blessings" that Lydia showered on him that day.

Tales from the Tureks

Chuck and Nancy Turek lived five houses to the west of John and Lydia from 1984 until 1999. Nancy can tell many wonderful stories about Lydia, who seemed to be everybody's parent on the road and everybody's friend. Lydia was the "road guard" on Roots Beach Lane, a private drive with 18 houses on the lake side that dead-ends. Lydia monitored all the traffic and was the ruling force. It was not uncommon for her to stop traffic and tell drivers to slow down on that 15-mile-per-hour stretch. Strangers might be asked what they were doing there.

Chuck and Nancy, as well as neighbors DeBlonde and Mary Johnson, had no basements. Whenever there were tornado warnings, which happened occasionally in the spring and summer, they ran down the road with their children to John and Lydia's house. Lydia's house was a walk-through, but the dirt was landscaped to the second story on both the west and east sides, so the first floor was safe. Lydia brewed coffee and they played cards until the warning expired.

Although Lydia was old enough to be Nancy's mother, Nancy says Lydia was always young at heart. Both Nancy and Lydia's brother Adi were terrified of snakes. Lydia had a box with an artificial snake coiled inside. Once when Adi was visiting and watching, Lydia handed the box to Nancy. When she opened it, the coiled snake shot out. Nancy and Adi were horrified.

Everybody who became a friend of Lydia was a friend forever. Chuck and Nancy played cards with Lydia and John four to six evenings a week. It was always girls against the guys and they kept track of who won on the calendar. Of all the years they played, the men only won one year. At the end of each year that the women won, Nancy made a necklace out of the calendar and wore it when they played. Usually they played 500, but sometimes euchre.

In the summer, campfires behind the Johnson house were frequent. Neighbors brought over chairs when they saw the fires burning, and they drank beer and wine and told jokes and stories. John and Lydia were usually there.

The property across the road from the homes on Roots Beach Lane is owned by the state Department of Natural Resources (DNR). Nancy and Lydia once planted 200 evergreen trees in those woods to help replace some that had been lost in a flood. Lydia complained about the DNR because she thought they were disrupting the birds and frogs in the area.

After Lydia retired, she and John went almost daily for years to Fisher's Corner Bar for breakfast with Woody and Betty Palmer,

Bob and Ruby Cumberland, Bill and Grace Roberts, Joe and Nadine Strong, and Buster Verschoor. After coming home, Lydia put the coffee pot on for the neighbors at the lake. Millie Roemhildt was another dear friend with whom Lydia enjoyed playing the card game hand and foot.

Thoughts from the Thayers

Scott and Ginger Thayer lived next door to the west for two months after their marriage on March 22, 1980. They remember Lydia's wonderful hospitality, receiving a prize fern peony root from her, and feeding the fish from her dock.

Tamara Thayer lived in the same house with her husband, David, for a couple years after their marriage in November 1985. Tammy recalled the many walks Lydia took with her when Tammy's pregnancy was past its due date in September 1987. Lydia thought the walks would help start the labor process. She always told Tammy to ensure that the nurses checked the afterbirth to determine that all of it was there, so Tammy did not end up so sick like Lydia after childbirth and not able to have more children.

In January 2008, Dave and Edna Thayer left on a 10-day trip to a warmer climate. On Saturday night, the temperature dropped to over 20 degrees below zero. Lydia recalled that the previous year when Dave and Edna were away, their water pipes had frozen. Being a caring and thoughtful neighbor and wanting to prevent that from happening again, Lydia telephoned the chief City Engineer John Roessler on Sunday morning and asked him to come to the Thayer house to flush the water line. Because it would do no good to tell her that that was not part of his job description, John came to the Thayer house on that Sunday morning and did what was necessary to ensure that the water in the pipes would continue to flow. This could happen only in a small town like Elysian and with an assertive and attentive neighbor like Lydia. It also helped to have an accommodating chief city engineer.

Happenings from the Hauses

Emery and Betty Haus moved into the house on the east side of the Rosses in 1982. Lydia welcomed them with a hug, a smile, and her heavy German accent. She invited them often for supper and usually served the hot German potato salad for which she was famous. The evenings were typically filled with games of 500 and stories of Lydia's life in Germany. Sometimes Lydia and Emery clashed during the bidding, and Lydia would have a choice name for him in jest, but the evening always ended happily, often with angel food cake, lemon topping, and Cool Whip. She also had German chocolate candy made with different varieties of alcohol inside as a special treat.

The coffee pot was always on, and there were often German cookies. Lydia was generous with her flowers and vegetables, especially her prize tomatoes. Fern peonies filled her garden in early spring. Lydia kept her spade handy so she could dig a root for a friend. "You only get one root, so take care of it!" she warned.

In 1985 Betty and Emery traveled to Hannibal, Mo., with John and Lydia. Lydia helped the time pass with her storytelling. They visited Julia Fuller, who had sold Emery and Betty their cabin. They took a day trip to St. Louis and rode to the top of the Gateway Arch. Lydia and John became frightened in the small elevator, and John cried loudly, "I gotta get out of here! Get me down!" The elevator stopped instantly. There was a camera inside it, and workers from the arch were operating the controls. When they heard John they stopped the elevator. Lydia said, "Oh, he's OK; keep going." So they continued to the top.

Snippets from the Steiners

In 2000, when Jim and Betty Steiner bought a home six houses west of John and Lydia, they were told that Roots Beach had its own unofficial mayor whose name was Lydia. Obviously the mayor was also traffic cop. Lydia and John's home sat on the curve of Roots Beach Lane, so they had a clear view of cars and people going back and forth on the road. Their chairs faced the road and not the lake, unlike most of the neighbors'. Here Lydia could watch over her garden and the birds in her feeders. Lydia sat close enough to the road that she could run out waving her arms and in no uncertain words inform friend and foe alike that 15-miles-per-hour was the absolute speed limit on Roots Beach Lane – so slow down! Lydia enjoyed having people stop to visit and had nicknames for everyone living on the lane, such as "Fifty Trips."

Jim remembers that once when Dave and Edna Thayer were away on a short vacation and he was watching the house, he decided to park his pickup in the Thayer's driveway to give the impression that someone was at home. Jim left on a business trip for a few days, and when he returned, Lydia in her feisty manner informed him that the truck blocked her view of the road. Lydia demanded that Jim remove it immediately and he complied. Lydia did not realize that the keys were in the truck and that either she or John could have moved it.

Lydia and Francine, Jim and Betty's poodle, had a mutual admiration society. Francine enjoyed walking down the road on her own to visit and Lydia showered her with affection and doggie treats.

Jim and Betty enjoyed taking John and Lydia on a pontoon ride each summer, hearing Lydia's jokes, and eating treats on the boat. Lydia gave a guided tour, as she knew all the residents around the lake as well as their history. Lydia's feast of German radish or kohlrabi sandwiches on German sourdough bread, washed down with German Oktoberfest beer, provided a gourmet experience like no other.

Now when Jim and Betty drive by and glance at the house with their memories of John and Lydia sitting outside, it saddens them. Betty treasures the memories she has when she looks at her fern peony, a special gift from Lydia.

SUMMARY

Lydia had a reputation for being a very social, caring, and sharing person. She was a lot of fun, and often had a cute story or joke to tell. Yes, she was opinionated and did not hesitate to tell one what she thought. But when that happened, friends just shrugged their shoulders and said, "That's Lydia!"

A birthday party for Lydia
Notice the saying on Lydia's T-shirt.

CHAPTER 34

Jottings from John Jr.

*Each day of our lives we make deposits
in the memory banks of our children.*

Charles R. Swindoll

Johnny remembers a time when life was simpler and safer. He said that although his parents never had much money, they were good parents and provided what was needed. He said he treasures his memories of being a Mama's boy. Some of Johnny's other memories include:

John put a water line into their house in the city of Elysian. Lydia was often impatient to finish things, and she thought John was taking too long to refill the trench with dirt to cover the pipe. Lydia recruited some friends to help shovel. Johnny was playing with trucks on the dirt pile. One strong woman, Maggie Kline, thought he was in the way, so she hit him on the butt with the shovel to encourage him to stay back. Johnny said he got even with her a few days later. They were at the beach, and Johnny was swimming. He pretended to drown, and Maggie jumped in, clothes and all, to save him. She was not too happy when Johnny admitted that he was playing a prank. I wonder where Johnny developed that mischievous streak.

Johnny has no memories of life on the farm, but he does have memories of the farm after they moved to town, during the four years before his grandfather died in the hunting accident. He helped pick up corn and bales of hay. He was paid four cents a bale.

Once when they went to the farm to visit, Lydia told John, "Now, if they ask us to stay for supper, don't accept, because they always serve spaghetti or pancakes." So when Grandma Frances invited them to stay, as she often did, Johnny said, "No, we can't, because you always serve spaghetti or pancakes." (Never say anything in front of a child that you do not want to hear repeated.) Johnny also remembers the mush Frances frequently made for breakfast. Although he does not know exactly what it was, he remembers that he did not like the taste.

Once, Johnny's grandfather left a pair of knee-high boots in an old shed near their house. Johnny said there were many small, strange old sheds on their land and that Lydia tired of looking at them. She sometimes lit fire to a shed and burned it to the ground just to remove it from the property. She decided to do that to the shed that contained Fred's boots. As luck would have it, he came looking for his boots soon after Lydia had burned them. Lydia said that the shed accidentally caught on fire and that the boots must have gone up in smoke with it.

When Johnny was about four, he was kicked in the head by one of Fred's horses. He passed out, but was not seriously injured. John also had horses, and shortly after that accident, John and Johnny decided to sell them to buy a boat and motor for fishing and a couch for Lydia. Johnny and his dad often fished. When Johnny was preschool age, all the fishing sometimes bored him. Once when they were fishing on Lake Francis by Willow Point, across the lake and several blocks from home, Johnny complained of being tired and said he wanted to quit. John crossed the lake and left Johnny off on shore and told him to walk home. Another time they were near Clarke's campground, over a mile from the house, and Johnny said he wanted to quit fishing. This time John told him he could swim to shore and walk home and Johnny did. Lydia was not too pleased. Despite the occasional boredom, Johnny acquired a love of fishing and hunting from his father.

Whenever Lydia started listening to Lawrence Welk or Liberace, two of her favorites, John would say to Johnny, "Let's go fishing." And they did.

Johnny was six when Fred died in 1953. Lydia decided to let him stay in school that day and did not tell him until he returned home. Some of Johnny's friends heard about the shooting on the radio when they went home for lunch, but they thought it was John who had died. They told Johnny that his father had died and Johnny thought his friends were playing a cruel joke and was very upset. When he came home from school, he learned it was his grandpa.

Johnny remembers the trip to Germany when he was nine and when grandfather Alois was dying of cancer. He and his grandfather played a lot of cards. Johnny remembers cheating, but like most young boys, he just wanted to win. He also remembers going to beer joints with Alois and being served a small glass of beer. Beer was delivered to German houses in the morning just like milk was delivered in America. One day Johnny went with a friend who was about 11 to deliver beer. At the end of the route, one container was left. Johnny said, "What should we do with that?" His friend replied, "Let's drink it." Johnny remembers feeling the effects when he returned to the house.

Johnny was almost 10 when he and Lydia returned from their trip to Germany. John was alternating working days and nights at Hubbard Milling in Mankato and Lydia was working the night shift at Munsingwear in Montgomery. Johnny stayed alone when both of his parents were at work. It was his job to do the dishes. He often fished to amuse himself. Spear fishing through the ice was popular during the winter. He took his spear to school and stored it in the hall. (Imagine taking a spear into school these days.) After school he went straight to the fish house. When he was 10 and 11, he and his friend pitched a tent in the summers to catch bullheads, clean them, and fry them for supper. Sometimes they hopped on the freight train that ran through town and rode to Waterville, six miles away. They hitchhiked home.

Johnny said there were many businesses in Elysian: a hotel, dance hall, creamery, elevator, two grocery stores, three gas stations, a hardware store, lumberyard, bank, two cafes, a hatchery, a construction company, and a doctor's office. On Saturday nights, free movies were shown on the side of a building outdoors. His parents popped corn and gave him a nickel to buy soda pop.

Once when Johnny was angry with his parents, he said he was leaving home. Lydia replied, "Good, I think we will go to a movie in Waterville tonight." Johnny wanted to see the movie, so of course he changed his mind about leaving and they all went to the movie. He knew that was Lydia's way of getting him to change his mind. John often lost his billfold in the theater because it fell out of his pocket when he sat. They were usually partway home before John realized it was missing—probably when they were deciding whether to stop for a snack. Stopping for ice cream was always a special treat. Johnny knew better than to ask, but he always hoped they would stop. He remembers that all three of them could get a hamburger and malt for $1 at Hattie's.

One year Lydia decided to raise chickens in their old six-by-eight fish house that they stored on their land in town. They bought 200 chickens. Johnny thinks most of them lived. Lydia sold half the chickens, gave a few to friends, and ate the rest. Johnny remembers helping to kill the chickens, removing the feathers, and cleaning out the insides. They ate chicken every which way: baked and fried, and in soup, sandwiches, stews, salads, and hot dishes. To this day, neither John nor Johnny cares much for chicken.

Lydia taught Johnny to play many card games. Johnny said that she never let him win because he had to learn to play well enough to win on his own. When he did learn to win, Lydia sometimes got so upset that she threw the cards at him.

Lydia really wanted a china cabinet. The town barber was planning to drive the 70 miles to the Twin Cities to purchase items at an auction in an old hotel. Lydia asked him to buy a china cabinet

Johnny and Diane

if he found one for sale. Johnny said the barber brought a huge black one home that cost $20. John was not happy, because he earned only $40 a week. Lydia and Johnny refinished the cabinet. It took a week to strip. When Johnny burned the rags in the garbage, there was an explosion, and his hands were badly burned.

Some years later, Johnny took the cabinet to the woodworking shop at the Waterville school to refinish it. It was a nice maple wood. Its glass mirror was large and thick. When they tried to cut the mirror down, it broke, but they replaced it with a smaller, nicer mirror. The china cabinet has become a treasured antique and is still being used in the family by grandson Kirk.

Johnny was a sophomore in high school in 1962 when his parents bought the lake home. He lived there five years until he married Diane Cowdin on September 19, 1967. Johnny and his friends enjoyed the lake activities of water skiing, swimming, fishing, and boating.

Johnny said his parents continued attending the high school games long after he graduated, until John's knees started to bother him and he did not feel like walking as much. He parked in a handicapped spot without a permit and received a ticket. They stopped going to the games.

Johnny said no one ever had to wonder what his mother was thinking. She always told you.

Johnny and Diane with Kirk and Christine, 1976

CHAPTER 35

Kernels from Kirk and Kin

Grandchildren are God's way of compensating for us growing old.

Mary H. Waldrip

Kirk Ross, Lydia's oldest grandchild and only grandson, has fond memories of his childhood when he lived in the same town as his grandparents. He and his family were pleased to share fond recollections of Lydia.

Feisty is the perfect word—so small physically, but yet that little "kraut," as my grandfather affectionately called her, packed the heart of a lion. She would have given you the shirt off her back if you were in trouble. She could also rip it off you if you were the one causing the trouble. It would be best to be on her team, as opposition was usually futile. I learned this many times trying to test her. If she were set on something and had her mind made up, you were not going to swing her. We always called her the "soup" (supervisor). Dad and I always marveled at her ability to give direction and guidance on most any project. My grandfather was always being supervised. I know for a fact he would not have had it any other way.

Kirk remembers sitting in the Jeep with John on Friday nights waiting for Lydia to come home from E F Johnson after working hard all week. He always jumped around, excited to see her. It was *Dukes of Hazzard, Dallas,* and pizza at Grandma's on Friday nights. Kirk loved the lake, where he could fish, swim, boat, and ride a snowmobile. The simple things were the best. Kirk said just being around his grandmother was entertaining enough. No television comedy was needed.

Lydia's English was generally good, although she struggled with a few words. Kirk remembers her talking about "Richy Call" all the time. She would say, "I spoke with Richy Call the other day," or "Richy Call phoned me and we spoke for hours." Kirk wondered why he had never met this person who seemed to be so much a part of his grandmother's life. He knew that Lydia's good friends next to the Ross farm had the last name Call. He said he must have been 12 before he realized that Richy Call was not a person. Lydia could not pronounce "whatchamacallit," so she just said, "Richy Call."

My grandma was well endowed. One time I was showering in the bathroom as a young kid. With soap in my eyes, I reached for a towel and grabbed what I thought was a towel. Much to my surprise, my entire face and head fit inside one of the large cups of her bra. I shrieked, "Ahhhhhh!" She asked me why I was yelling. I said, "Grandma, I almost lost my head in that bra." I also remember her reading books to me as a small child while I sat on her lap. This was long before I really knew what boobs were. I thought Grandma had such great built-in pillows.

Kirk believes the greatest legacy Lydia will leave is her feisty spirit. Her love for life and people was evident every day. Kirk says the feistiness is alive and well within him, and he believes it has contributed to his success. He is grateful for it. While he teases his sister for having their grandmother's spirit, he is aware that the apple did not fall far from the tree and that he also has that spirit. He even notices it in Lydia's young great-grandchildren. Kirk is pleased that this book was written to celebrate his grandmother. Just as Lydia's spirit is being passed from generation to generation, this book can be passed down so the grandchildren, their children, and their children's children can learn about that special lady, Lydia, and know why they are special, too.

Kirk's wife, Lisa, says there was never a dull moment around Lydia. The words that came out of her mouth were always entertaining and always good for a laugh. Lydia talked a lot about what was going on in Elysian, as she was always in the know. Lisa says she always felt at home in Lydia's house and that Lydia spoiled her more than Kirk did. (She was quick to add that Kirk was OK with that). Lisa has fond memories of playing the card game hand and foot with Lydia. They played for hours. With three decks of cards, it was a challenge to keep them shuffled. Lydia always asked Lisa if she cheated; which she did not, but if she picked up a foot or went out, Lydia shouted, "Lisa!"

Toads came out at night from the black swamp across the road from Lydia's home to feed on bugs under the light outside the garage and to seek warmth from the driveway. When Kirk and Lisa were dating and leaving the house at night, there were often hundreds of jumping toads. Lydia would hear Lisa shriek and told Kirk to carry her and stop teasing her. Lydia dearly loved her family and was very protective of them. Lisa said they all loved her dearly in return for how she blessed their lives with zest and humor. Kirk and Lisa married on October 14, 1989.

Grandson Kirk, wife Lisa, and children Karlie and Caleb

Great-grandchildren Karlie was born on April 4, 1994, and Caleb was born on January 26, 1998. They wrote:

We always enjoyed feeding Oma's school of sunfish that lived under her dock. She would give us bread to feed them. When they heard us come walking onto the dock, they would swim out and wait for us to throw the bread. Oma loved to give big hugs and she always gave us a cold soda and the big-size candy bars. Yummy! When we were small she was so proud to swing us on the little yellow swing hanging under her deck. We loved to play with the duck decoys and toys at the lake. Oma was so proud of the many birds at the lake. She had ducks, wrens, martins, and trumpeter swans that would all come to her house. We would feed corn to the swans and ducks. Oma also had the best cherry tomatoes from her garden and flowers that were really unique. We loved to smell the flowers. She has given us some of those flower bulbs that we have planted at our house in Lakeville. She was our great-grandmother, but we always called her Oma, the German word for grandma. She was a great oma! Thanks for all the memories, Oma!

Love, Karlie and Caleb.

Lydia with Caleb and Karlie in the hospital when Caleb was born

CHAPTER 36

Comments from Christine

*The person one becomes depends on
the person one has been.*

Dick Francis

Lydia always wanted more children, but could not have them, so she was especially fond of her two grandchildren who grew up in Elysian. Christine is the second grandchild and only granddaughter. She was pleased to share comments about life with Grandma Lydia.

> *When I thought about your title,* Feisty Lydia, *I couldn't help but agree that you could not have picked a better title. That pretty much sums her up in a phrase. It's funny, because my brother, Kirk, always laughs at me and smiles when he says, "The older you get, the more like Grandma you become. When you're older you'll be just like her." What is funny about that is he usually says it right after I have acted or behaved in a way that might be described as feisty. I think I have inherited or learned some of that behavior. Actually, I have put it to good use in my life. (Thank you, Grandma.)*

Christine recalls many times when her grandmother took charge of situations in surprising ways. Once when Christine was young, Lydia strongly reprimanded a waitress for not bringing the dessert quickly enough. Lydia had seen the girl chatting with co-workers and thought she was neglecting her job. Lydia had a suggestion or two for the young woman.

Grandma Lydia always told Christine about her love for dancing while growing up in Germany. Even though Emilie worried about

Lydia being out at night during the war, Lydia would sneak out of the house late to go dancing. More than once, Emilie pulled Lydia out of the dance hall by her hair to take her home. Lydia would go to her room, wait for the house to get quiet, and back out she would go, determined to enjoy her favorite pastime.

Christine fondly recalls her grandparents' longtime support of the school sports teams. They were usually in the stands for the Friday night football games and in the bleachers for the basketball games. Once, Christine went with them to a boys' basketball championship game. Waterville won, and afterward John got the car stuck in a snow bank in the parking lot. Lydia and Christine got out of the car to push. Lydia pushed with all her might, and she lost her footing, slipped, and went down. Because Lydia was not hurt, the sight of her 60-year-old grandmother lying in the snow, partway underneath the car, made Christine laugh uncontrollably. Christine suspects Lydia was not laughing with her.

When Christine was about 15, she took a road trip with John and Lydia to South Dakota to tour such sights as the Black Hills and Mount Rushmore. After a couple days of touring, Christine suggested that they do a teenage activity by eating pizza and going to a movie. John and Lydia agreed and they went to a Pizza Hut. Seated next to them were a group of people speaking Spanish. After they left the restaurant, Lydia was annoyed that people living in America were not speaking English. Christine said she argued with her, because at age 15 one knows everything, and tried to explain that they may not have known English and they had a right to speak whatever language they wanted over their dinner. Christine says she believes it was Lydia's love for America that was behind her objections.

Lydia struggled hard to learn English after she came "over the pond." Once she mistakenly bought SOS scrubbing pads because she read the initials as one word and thought it was "sauce." Christine says she knows our experiences shape our perspectives in life, and even though she did not always agree with Lydia, she respected her.

Lydia with "the men" at Christine's wedding

The day Stephen and I were married was October 11, 1997. We chose this date because we love the fall and wanted a nice cool day. Stephen is from Scotland, and he and his groomsmen would be wearing kilts – warm, wool kilts. Well, as Minnesota weather would have it, it was 80 degrees that day. The boys were hot in the church basement, where they had gone to try to stay cool. And where was Grandma on my wedding day? She was with the guys in the basement. She had heard a rumor that men do not wear underwear under their kilts, and she wanted to see if there was any truth to it. So down she went to charm the boys and try to sneak a peek. Stephen says that she said, "You know, I'm wearing shiny shoes, and when they are strategically placed, I might be able to get a reflection."

The final thing I remember about Grandma is her involvement in my life. She came to all my activities, plays, music, concerts, and sporting events. She was my fan, my supporter, and my friend. She was always proud of me, and I always knew it, as did the rest of the town.☺ There was nowhere we could go that we did not run into someone Grandma knew or someone who knew her. When one met Lydia, she always made an impression. She was the kind of woman whom people do not easily forget. I will always fondly remember the positive impact Grandma had on my life.

Lydia was very proud of her five great-grandchildren. Christine and Stephen have three children. The oldest, Ian, was born on May 1, 2003. His name is Scottish for John and means "God's gracious gift." The second, Evan, was born on November 6, 2005. His name is Welsh for John and means "God is good." Evan in Celtic means "young warrior." Christine jokingly says that it must translate into English as "feisty," because he has a strong will just like his Oma Lydia. Ayla was born February 3, 2008. The Scottish spelling of her name, Aila, means "from the strong place." The spelling Ayla, is Hebrew for Oak tree. Both represent strength. Lydia was quick to tell you that both Ian and Evan are other names for John.

John and Lydia with their five great-grandchildren
Ayla, Karlie, Caleb, Evan, and Ian
Thanksgiving, 2008

Great grandchildren Ian & Evan

Four generations—Lydia with her youngest great grandchild,
Thanksgiving, 2008, left to right: Ayla Mae Paton,
Christine Paton, Diane Ross, Lydia Ross

Stephen and Christine Paton, Ayla Mae, Ian, and Evan,
Christmas, 2008

RETIREMENT

YEARS

John and Lydia in retirement
Who's the German?

Lydia behind the wheel of her new car

CHAPTER 37

Getting Her Driver's License

*Lydia's biggest driving problem was remembering to
open the garage door before backing out.*

John Ross

When Lydia retired in 1986 at 61, her friend Norma Seifert encouraged her to get a driver's license so she could go where she wanted in retirement. She took profit-sharing money she had earned and bought a new shiny red Pontiac Grand Prix.

Lydia had previously owned another car, an old used Buick she purchased in 1960. She and 13-year-old Johnny tried to learn to drive that car. They were lucky she bought it. One day John Sr. left his keys in his car at work in Mankato, and when he left work to go home, the car was missing. Lydia asked a neighbor to drive her old Buick to Mankato to get John. Later John's car was found parked elsewhere in town, out of gas, but unharmed.

John took Lydia to the farm to teach her to drive. During her first lesson, John got out of the car and told her to drive it up closer to the house, but he forgot to tell her how to stop the car. She was going slowly and drove it into a tree to stop. The car was undamaged.

Johnny recalls the day Lydia stopped driving until she retired. Both Johnny and Lydia drove the Buick around town. Back then, a test was not required for a license. One could just buy a license for $3 at the bank. John and Lydia did not want to spend the money, so Lydia drove without a license. One day Johnny was a passenger when a police officer stopped Lydia and asked her if she had a license. Lydia told him, "You know I don't." The policeman said, "Then I will have to give you a ticket." When he handed it to Lydia, she said, "What am I supposed to do with this?" He replied, "You can wipe your butt with it if you want to." Lydia drove a couple blocks away, and threw the ticket out the window. Johnny said they never heard another word about it. Lydia stopped driving until after she retired.

After retirement, the first time Lydia took her driver's test, she went through a stop sign and the test was stopped. The next time, she checked out the route in advance for stop signs, but the examiner went a different route. She passed anyway.

Lydia mostly drove within a 20-mile radius of Elysian. She was a safe and cautious driver. Her biggest problem was remembering to open the garage door before backing out. She hit the door three times with the car. The first two times there was no damage. The third time the door had to be replaced and the car was damaged. Lydia owned three new Pontiacs after retirement, two red and one green.

Lydia bringing home a German doll from one of her flights back home

CHAPTER 38

Only Lydia Could

If God had wanted me to be otherwise,
He would have created me otherwise.

Johann von Goethe

John and Lydia returned together to visit Germany four times. Lydia also returned with Johnny when her father was dying of cancer, and another time with her brother, Adi.

On one of their later trips home from Germany, John and Lydia were running late at the airport in Kansas where they needed to transfer planes. While Lydia went to the desk to make arrangements about the tickets, John laid his medications down on the counter and had a cigarette. Lydia asked when the plane was leaving and was informed that it was backing away. Lydia and John ran outside, and Lydia frantically waved to the pilot to stop for them. He did, and they boarded the plane.

After John and Lydia were seated, John's eyes filled with tears. Lydia thought he was just exhausted from running to catch the plane, but she asked him what was wrong. He said he had left his medications on the counter inside the airport.

Lydia raced to the cockpit and told the pilot he had to turn around so John could get his medications (this was back when the cockpit door was often left open). They were needed for heart problems and diabetes. The pilot phoned the desk inside the terminal and was told that the medicines were indeed there. Once again he returned to the gate, where an airlines employee met them with the bag of medicine.

Only Lydia could get a pilot of a major airline to turn a plane around to come back—and not once, but twice—before ever leaving the ground.

Neighbor Brenda Thayer chipping a souvenir
for Lydia from the Berlin Wall
November 9, 1989

CHAPTER 39

Lydia Comments on the Berlin Wall

The wall came tumbling down.

Jeff Jacoby, Boston Globe staff

Lydia shared her thoughts about the Berlin Wall. When the wall was built, it was erected with no choice of where one would reside. Family members were separated. The brother-in-law of Lydia's brother was a dentist in East Germany. It was difficult for family members to cross to visit each other.

Economic times were not as good for the people of East Germany. Once, the dentist's mother baked a cake to send to him, with some gold baked inside. Perhaps the cake was a little heavy. It was opened at the border and confiscated. Another time Lydia's mother and sister went to visit their brother and sister, who would be Lydia's aunt and uncle, and who lived in East Germany. On their return, the young border guard who searched the car told them, "You'd have room in the trunk for me." Whether he was serious or not, the women did not risk it.

The results of the wall coming down were met with mixed emotion by the West Germans. It was great to freely cross and be able to be reunited with family and friends. However, many of the East Germans who fled over to West Germany after the wall came down had no jobs. The government helped them get reestablished and paid those people monthly checks. When they did get jobs, they sometimes took jobs that the West Germans also wanted. Although Lydia was pleased about the reunification, it was not uncommon for some of the West Germans and some of Lydia's relatives to wish that the Wall had stayed in place.

THE BERLIN WALL

The Berlin Wall was built in 1961 to prevent the citizens who resided in East Germany from crossing over to West Germany. Following the war, the West German people made a remarkable recovery and their economy quickly improved. This was not happening under the authoritarian government in East Germany. Many people tried to defect. After the wall was built, at least 136 were killed attempting to cross the border from East to West Germany. The wall was up for 28 years and one day, and began to come down in 1989. German reunification formally concluded on October 3, 1990.

CHAPTER 40

It's a Small, Small World

Though the mountains divide and the oceans are wide,
It's a small, small world.

Disney

Lydia thought the air force lieutenant who had given her the dress uniform that hung in her closet in Germany was nice. He was also handsome with blond hair and blue eyes. She had met him while attending beauty school and they dated a couple times before he left. When he was transferred, he left his dress uniform with Lydia because he could not take it with him. They corresponded frequently. He mailed her things from Italy, such as material for clothes and leather gloves. He also mailed an 8-by-10 photo with "Urchin, Nice meeting you, Otto" written on the back. When translated into English, urchin means mischievous child.

When Otto received the dress uniform from Lydia, he misinterpreted her reason for returning it and believed any possible romance was over. He stopped corresponding with her.

Over 50 years later, in the spring of 1997, Waterville High School had a German exchange student, Stephen Wunderlich. The director of the exchange program, Sonia Ziemer, lives on Lake Francis. Stephen stayed with the Ziemers at the end of his exchange program. Sonia brought him to meet Lydia and reminisce about Germany.

When Lydia learned that Stephen was from Berlin, she asked him if he could check the phone book when he returned to see if Otto still lived there. Stephen found Otto living only 2 blocks away in Berlin. Stephen went to see him and told him about Lydia. Otto said he wanted to hear from Lydia, and he gave his address to Stephen, who sent it to Lydia.

Lydia was thrilled. She checked her old photo album filled with pictures of soldiers she had known and found a large picture of Otto, along with some smaller ones. She mailed them to him along with a letter and an update on her life.

Otto was not well enough to write himself, so his daughter wrote to Lydia. His son and grandson were especially pleased to receive the photos, as they were pictures of Otto in the service that the family did not have. Lydia learned all about his family. After over fifty years of no contact, it is indeed a small, small world.

Lydia's tomato plants are taller than she is, 2005

CHAPTER 41

Enjoying Life at Le Center Central Health Care

Love is a game that two can play and both win.

Eva Gabor

Health problems, including open heart surgery, knee surgeries, and diabetes, eventually forced John to move into the Le Center Central Health Care nursing home in February 2005. Although John liked it there, he was very unhappy being without Lydia and begged her to take him home whenever she came to visit. She did attempt to take him home several times, but could not take care of him. He fell and needed help getting up. By then Lydia was on dialysis. Being petite anyway, and needing to protect the shunts in her arms, Lydia could not lift him into a standing position. Family and neighbors tried to help, but they were not always available.

In April 2008 Lydia's diabetes had become unstable. She would suffer insulin reactions and feared that she would lose consciousness and that no one would find her. She was also on dialysis three times a week. She decided to enter Le Center Central Health Care to be with John and receive the care she needed. She was given a bed in a room with John. The two single beds were moved together to form one large bed. That also left more space in the room.

In May 2008 John and Lydia were proud to be named the year's king and queen of the nursing home. Selecting a king and queen is an annual event held during nursing home week.

John and Lydia could not have been happier. Once again they were together and sharing life. They were quick to praise the staff and the conditions at the home. Lydia said the employees were friendly and helpful, the food was good, and there were a lot of activities to occupy their time. Lydia no longer had the worry of maintaining the home on Lake Francis and living alone. John was taking two fewer pills a day that had been prescribed for anxiety and depression. Both were content.

Lydia and John as queen and king
Nursing Home Week, May 2008
Central Health Care, Le Center, Minnesota

CHAPTER 42

The Roof Comes Tumbling Down

Wise men never sit and wail their loss,
but cheerily seek how to redress their harms.

William Shakespeare

In the summer of 2008, John had left the room to go to breakfast in another wing of the center where the residents dined. Lydia always preferred to sleep through breakfast and eat later in her room.

Lydia awoke to the noise of a strong storm. There was a heavy downpour of rain and strong straight-line winds. Suddenly the roof collapsed above her with a chunk of roof and torrents of rain landing hardest on John's bed next to hers. Although the storm was not classified as a tornado, it was close to one. Lydia could have been badly injured if the roof had fallen on her side of the bed.

The staff quickly ushered the residents into a waiting room, forgetting about Lydia back in her wing. She got out of bed and waded through the foot of water in the room. She made it to the door and shouted for help. The staff eventually heard her and came to take her to the safety of the other wing.

It took a little over a month to repair the roof and damage to the room. During this time John and Lydia were able to share a room, although it was much smaller than the one they had had before. After the roof was repaired, they were moved back to their original room.

The good news from the event was that John received a new chair. He had had one with an automatic lift built in to help him into a standing position. It was damaged in the storm, but the insurance company paid for a new one, which cost $800.

John and Lydia's silver anniversary celebration, August 1972
Celebrated early so family could be present.
L-R, standing: Sister Elfriede and husband Roland from Indiana
Sister Anne and husband Martin from Canada
Lydia and John
Sitting: Brother Adolf from Prior Lake, Minnesota

CHAPTER 43

Update on Lydia's Herman Family

God gave us our memories so that we might have roses in December.

James M. Barrie

What happened to the members of Lydia's family after she left Germany?

Lydia's sister Elfriede married an American soldier shortly after Lydia left Germany. She first lived in California where her husband was stationed. Soon after she came to America, she visited John and Lydia in Elysian. Lydia served goulash and ice cream. Elfriede enjoyed the ice cream so much that she wanted Lydia to send some back with her to California, not realizing it would melt on the way. During the night she was hungry and wanted to snack on the leftover goulash, but she could not find it in the refrigerator. The next morning she asked Lydia where it was. Lydia told her she had fed the leftovers to the dog. Elfriede said, "I'm going to tell Mama on you. She would not like to see you waste food." Elfriede and her husband lived most of their life in Frankfort, Indiana. She has since died.

Lydia's sister Anne moved to Canada. A friend in a butcher shop in Germany had received a letter from relatives on a farm in Canada. They wondered if someone would be willing to come to Canada to marry their son. Anne thought it would be an adventure

*Lydia (on right) visiting in Germany
with brother Seigfried and his wife, Edith*

and she accepted the offer. They were happy together and had seven children.

The first time brother Adi came to North America was to work on the railroad near Anne in Canada. He was unhappy there and decided to return to Germany. Later, in 1962, he came to Elysian to help John and Lydia move into their new home on Lake Francis. John and Lydia had to sign for him to come to America and got a job for him working on the highway in Minneapolis, where Johnny also worked in the summer. Adi liked the Twin Cities and married a woman with five children. One already had a child, so Adi became an instant grandfather. Adi lives in Burnsville, 50 miles from Elysian. He visited Lydia often, especially during the summer when he could ride his motorcycle. When Adi was asked to recall

Standing: Brother Adolf, niece Lydia, Lydia Ross
Sitting, sister Elfriede, sister Luise, mother of niece Lydia

memories of Lydia in Germany, he said he wanted to forget the war years and being hungry. He is an American now and he loves this country. This is what he wants to remember.

Lydia's siblings Carl, Seigfried, and Luise remained in Germany. Carl and Luise have both died.

Alois died of cancer in 1957. With her husband gone and half her children living in America, Emilie decided to come to the United States. Lydia had sent her money once before to come for a visit. When Emilie was 65, she came back a second time, for her birthday. She loved John and Lydia's lake home and planned to stay.

While Emilie was in Elysian in 1965, Elfriede's husband in Indiana needed to be at a camp in Wisconsin for two weeks. They asked Emilie to come to Indiana to visit and help Elfriede with the children. Elfriede's husband came to Minnesota to take her to Indiana. On a six-lane highway in Hammond, Indiana, Lydia's mother died in a horrific car crash. She was flown back to the mortuary in Waterville, Minnesota, and was buried next to John's parents at the Cedar Hill Cemetery in Elysian.

Lydia enjoying the flowers in her garden

CHAPTER 44

Secrets of Survival

There's a dark and a troubled side of life;
There's a bright and a sunny side, too.
Though we meet with the darkness and strife,
The sunny side we also may view.
Keep on the sunny side, always on the sunny side,
Keep on the sunny side of life.
It will help us every day, It will brighten all the way,
If we keep on the sunny side of life.

J. Howard Entwisle, 1890

How did Lydia survive a premature birth, the Great Depression, war in her hometown and country, several potentially deadly situations, tragedy, and a new life in a foreign country? The secrets of her survival are summarized through the acronym S-U-R-V-I-V-A-L.

S Spirit

U Understanding of Finances

R Religious Beliefs

V Values

I Industriousness

V Voice

A Attitude

L Laughter

S — Spirit

Nothing great was ever achieved without enthusiasm.
Ralph Waldo Emerson

Lydia was known for her high spirits and zest for life. In the positive meaning of the word, she was a feisty woman. People loved her enthusiasm and enjoyed being around her.

U — Understanding of Finances

This one makes a net, this one stands and wishes.
Would you like to make a bet which one gets the fishes?
Chinese rhyme

Although Lydia came to America not knowing the value of the currency, it did not take her long to learn. As someone who had lived through the world-wide Depression in Germany, she knew the value of money and how to survive on little. She was the one who could obtain bank loans and mortgages when needed, and she worked hard to pay them off, usually before the due date.

R — Religious Beliefs

God speaks to all individuals through what happens
to them moment by moment.
J. P. DeCaussade

Lydia was a devout Catholic and believed God had a hand in guiding her throughout her life. She believed she had a guardian angel who kept her from going to work at the munitions plant in Germany the day it was bombed and no one came out alive. Prayer helped her through many turbulent times.

V—Values

Those who bring sunshine to the lives of others
cannot keep it from themselves.
James Matthew Baerie

Family, friends, and country are among things that Lydia valued most in life. She was proud of her whole family and enjoyed being with them. She was sociable and also enjoyed being with friends. She valued both her native country of Bavaria and her adopted country of America.

I — Industriousness

There are no secrets to success.
It is the result of hard work.
General Colin Powell

Lydia worked hard all her life starting at age 14 in Germany. Except for short periods when she was in beauty school, after she had Johnny, and when it was difficult to find work, Lydia worked until she retired at age 61. Even then Lydia enjoyed working around the house and yard, and she kept vegetable and flower gardens until she entered the nursing home in 2008.

V—Voice

I speak truth, not so much as I would, but as much as I dare;
and I dare a little more, as I grow older.
Montaigne

Lydia spoke her mind freely and was not one to bottle things up inside. She voiced her opinion to public officials, family and friends.

A – Attitude

Optimism is a cheerful frame of mind that enables
a teakettle to sing, though in hot water up to its nose.
Harold Helfer

Optimism and hope were strong in Lydia. She did not believe in feeling sorry for herself, but set out to make life as pleasant as she could.

L – Laughter

Being happy doesn't mean that everything is perfect;
It means that you've decided to see beyond perfection.
Dian Ritter

Lydia had a great sense of humor and was able to find the humor in nearly every situation. She loved telling a good joke and hearing one from others. Laughter was a way for her to dump emotional garbage and move on with life. She was able to "keep on the sunny side of life."

Enjoying Lydia's Flowers
Niece Lydia Schmid from Germany and great-granddaughter Karlie Ross

Epilogue

Lydia created her Elysian Fields in the city of Elysian, Minnesota. Her feisty spirit delighted in family and friends, who in turn found joy in her. She found peace and a refuge in her gardens and the surrounding woods and lake with their birds and animals. She was quick to express her happiness about coming to America. In the sunset of her life, she found happiness and contentment with John in their new surroundings in the nursing home in Le Center. Lydia was a survivor. Her life is a lesson and a blessing to many.

Lydia died surrounded by her loved ones on Sunday, March 22, 2009, from complications resulting from a fall and a fractured hip suffered three days before. She was 83.

Lydia feeding the trumpeter swans on her lawn

Poem Tribute from the Memorial Folder for
Lydia's Funeral, March 26, 2009

My Garden

Carice Williams

My garden gives me so much joy.
When dear friends come to call,
I like to have them view my flowers
Along my garden wall.

I've buttercups as bright as gold,
Fern peonies of red.
While in the springtime tulips wear
Bright turbans on their head.

There are hollyhocks against a fence
And black-eyes Susans, too.
While pink geraniums raise their heads
To get a better view.

And in a corner daisies bloom
As brightly as the sun,
While violets in a shady nook
Look bashful, every one.

I share my gardens with my friends
That they might share with me
The joy I feel in growing flowers
That last in memory.

APPENDICES

Significant towns from Lydia's life
Illustrated in their general proximity to each other

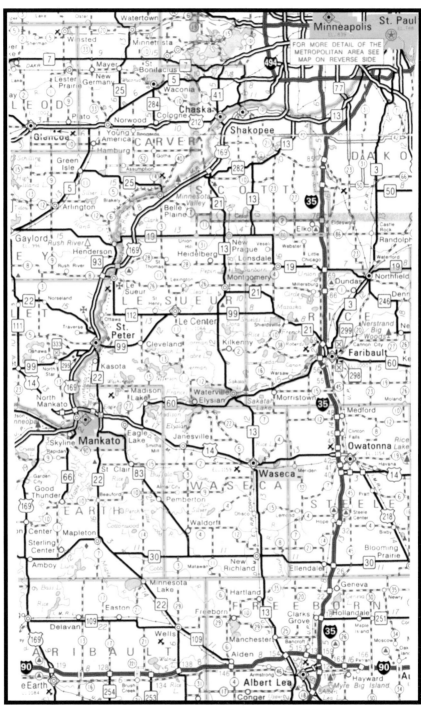

Significant towns in Lydia's corner of MN

Chronology of Lydia's Life

July 10, 1925 – Born prematurely; weighed 3 pounds.

1927-1931 – Attends preschool for four years.

1931-1939 – Attends school through eighth grade.

1939-1940 – Works in Munich.

1940-1941 – Attends beauty school in Altötting

1941-1943 – Works at an underground munitions plant in Kreiberg.

1944 – Works with an American medic group in Neuötting.

May 2, 1945 – War ends in Germany.

Summer 1945 – Meets John and works at The Club in Neuötting.

1946 – Works in Munich to be near John; becomes pregnant. Most of family has typhoid fever.

January 24, 1947 – Gives birth to Johnny Jr.

December 2, 1947 – Married twice, once by the American government and once by the German government.

December 3, 1947 – Married in the Catholic Church in Neuötting.

April 1, 1948 – John returns home to the farm in Elysian, Minnesota.

May 24, 1948 – Arrives in Elysian with Johnny Jr.

1950 – Buys a house in the city of Elysian. Works at Hattie's Restaurant.

1950-1952 – Works at Birdseye canning factory in Waseca.

1953-1963 – Works at Munsingwear in Montgomery.

1962 – Buys home on Lake Francis in Elysian.

1964-1986 – Works at E F Johnson in Waseca until retiring at age 61.

September 19, 1967 – Johnny Jr. marries Diane Cowdin.

April 18, 1972 – Granddaughter Christine Ross is born.

October 14, 1989 – Grandson Kirk marries Lisa Wermager.

April 4, 1994 – Great-granddaughter Karlie Ross is born.

October 11, 1997 – Granddaughter Christine marries Stephen Paton.

January 26, 1998 – Great-grandson Caleb Ross is born.

May 1, 2003 – Great-grandson Ian Paton is born.

February 2005 – John moves into nursing home in Le Center, Minnesota.

November 6, 2005 – Great-grandson Evan Paton is born.

February 3, 2008 – Great-granddaughter Ayla Mae Paton is born.

April 2008 – Lydia moves into nursing home sharing a room with John.

March 22, 2009 – Lydia dies from complications of a fall and broken hip.

Sources of Information

INTERVIEWS

Most of the information came directly from Lydia throughout the years since 1976. Other information came from interviews held with Lydia from the fall of 2008 through February 2009. John was present during most of the sessions and also contributed information.

Members of Lydia's family who were interviewed in January 2009 include her son, Johnny Jr.; his wife, Diane; Lydia's grandson, Kirk; his wife, Lisa; and their children, Karlie and Caleb; Lydia's granddaughter, Christine; and Lydia's brother Adi Weber.

Friends who were interviewed during January 2009 include Darlene Simons Adams, Brenda Eisenschenk, Betty and Emery Haus, Pat Nusbaum, Pat Quiram, Shirley Roemhildt, Norma Seifert, Stewart and Shirley Shaft, Marc Shaft, Mike Shaft, Scot Shaft, Shari Shaft Sneary, Stew Shaft II, Jim and Betty Steiner, Bob Tetzloff, Dave Thayer, Scott and Ginger Thayer, Tamara Thayer, Chuck and Nancy Turek, Carol Call Warweg, Herb Weber, and Sonia Ziemer.

BOOKS

Cook, John. *The Book of Positive Quotations*. Minneapolis, MN: Fairview Press, 1993.

Reader's Digest, *Quotable Quotes*. New York/Montreal: The Reader's Digest Association, 1997.

Ritter, Dian. *The Spice of Life*. Norwalk, CT: C. R. Gibson, Co. 1971.

The World Book Encyclopedia. Chicago: Field Enterprises Educational Corp., 1968.

ONLINE

http://elysian.com
(accessed January 2009)

http://en.wikipedia.org/wiki/Adolf_Hitler
(accessed December, 2008)

http://en.wikipedia.org/wiki/Bavaria/#History
(accessed January 2009)

http://en.wikipedia.org/wiki/Berlin_Wall
(accessed January, 2009)

http://en.wikipedia.org/wiki/Dachau_concentration_camp
(accessed December 2008)

http://en.wikipedia.org/wiki/List_of_cities_in_Germany
(accessed January 2009)

http://en.wikipedia.org/wiki/Paul_von_Hindenburg
(accessed December 2008)

http://en.wikipedia.org/wiki/Pope_Benedict_XVI
(accessed January 2009)

http://en.wikipedia.org/wiki/World_War_II
(accessed December 2008)

http://www.duchessathome.com/childrenssongs.html
(accessed January 2009)

http://www.kiddles.com/lyrics/s120.html
(accessed January 2009)

www.KeepOnTheSunnySide.com
(accessed January 2009)

About the Author

Edna Thayer

This is the third book authored by Edna Thayer since her retirement in 1996 after having worked as a nurse for over 40 years. The first, *Celebrating the First Fifty Years*, (2003), was co-authored by Dr. Mary Huntley and Linda Beer. It describes the history of the first 50 years of the nursing school at Minnesota State University, Mankato. The second book, *A Mirthful Spirit, Embracing Laughter for Wellness*, (2007), was co-authored by Dr. Mary Huntley. It describes the benefits of joy and laughter for health and wellness. Edna has a master's degree in nursing and a master's in counseling.

Feisty Lydia is Edna's first venture as a solo author. She married David Thayer on August 30, 1958. They bought the lake home next to John and Lydia Ross in 1976, living between Faribault and Elysian. They moved to the lake permanently in 1988. David and Edna have three children. Scott and Tammy both lived at the lake home for a short time after their marriages in 1980 and 1985 respectively. The youngest child, Brenda, had the most years to enjoy the lake. The entire family enjoyed knowing Lydia and being her neighbor.

About the Artist

Kirk Ross is the only grandson of John and Lydia. He was honored to create the wedding picture sketch of his grandparents that is on the cover of this book, and the map of Germany in the appendix. He is a graduate of Northwestern College in St. Paul, where he majored in graphic arts. He has done many illustrations over the past 20 years, along with some local artwork for the cities of Elysian and Waterville. The local designs included artwork for football signs and the Elysian centennial and redesigning the Buccaneer mascot for the Waterville-Elysian-Morristown schools. His current focus is sales and project design of recognition and award programs in Minneapolis for the Business Impact Group.

Kirk Ross

He is happily married to Lisa. They have two wonderful children, Karlie and Caleb. Kirk believes his life has been blessed by a great family and God's provisions.

Contact Information

To schedule a talk or purchase copies
of the book, contact the author at:

dethayer@myclearwave.net

www.feistylydia.com

info@feistylydia.com

Edna Thayer
7 Roots Beach Lane
Elysian, MN 56028
507-267-4588

Sun setting on Lake Francis
The view is to the west of Lydia's house.